Using Windows 3

Using Windows 3

Arthur Tennick

NEW TECH

Newtech
An imprint of Butterworth-Heinemann Ltd
Linacre House, Jordan Hill, Oxford OX2 8EJ

 PART OF REED INTERNATIONAL BOOKS

OXFORD   LONDON   BOSTON   MUNICH
NEW DELHI   SINGAPORE   SYDNEY
TOKYO   TORONTO   WELLINGTON

First published 1991
Reprinted 1991

© Arthur D. Tennick 1991

All rights reserved. No part of this publication may be reproduced in any material form (including photocopying or storing in any medium by electronic means and whether or not transiently or incidentally to some other use of this publication) without the written permission of the copyright holder except in accordance with the provisions of the Copyright, Designs and Patents Act 1988 or under the terms of a licence issued by the Copyright Licensing Agency Ltd, 33–34 Alfred Place, London WC1E 7DP, England.

Applications for the copyright holder's written permission to reproduce any part of this publication should be addressed to the publishers

British Library Cataloguing in Publication Data
A CIP catalogue record for this book is available from the British Library

ISBN 0 7506 0080 2

Printed and bound in Great Britain by
Biddles Ltd, Guildford and King's Lynn

Contents

Introduction ... 11

PART ONE — GETTING STARTED

1. Installing Windows 3 — 19
2. Starting Windows — 32
3. Printing from Windows — 36
4. Quitting Windows — 37
5. Essential skills — 40

PART TWO — ACCESSORIES

6. Using the accessories — 95
7. Applying the accessories — 98

PART THREE — MAIN GROUP AND PROGRAM MANAGER

8. File Manager — 131
9. Program Manager — 141
10. Print Manager — 147
11. Control Panel — 151
12. Clipboard — 163
13. DOS Icon — 164
14. Windows Setup — 165

PART FOUR — A CLOSER LOOK AT ACCESSORIES

15. More on accessories — 169
16. Cardfile — 170
17. Paintbrush — 178
18. Write — 188

PART FIVE — APPLICATIONS

19. Word Processors — 197
20. Desktop Publishing — 202
21. Spreadsheets — 204
22. Databases — 206
23. Graphics — 210

Contents

24	Time and project management	213
25	Development work	214
26	Fontware	216
27	UNIX links	218
28	Utilities	220

APPENDICES

A	Further accessories	225
B	Networks	228
C	Swapfiles	229

Index   235

Notes on the text

As far as possible the book contains practical exercises to help you become proficient in Windows 3. These exercises are in numbered steps. The text accompanying each step is indented. Some exercises continue over a number of pages and include other explanatory text. When such text is essential for the following steps it is also indented. The rest of the text in the exercises provides additional information which, although important, is not vital to subsequent steps. This text is not indented. Therefore it is possible to work quickly through the book by reading the indented text only.

The text was prepared in Word for Windows. Screen-shots were captured into Paintbrush via Clipboard in BMP format and saved out as PCX files. Initial layout of pages was created in PageMaker version 3.01, and proofed on a printer. The final CRC (*camera ready copy*) involved placing the text and screen-shots directly into Ventura Publisher (Windows version), and printing out on a PostScript laser printer. All the work in producing the final CRC was accomplished solely with Windows 3 and Windows 3-based applications.

The computer used was a 386 machine with 4 megabytes of RAM. The printer was a Panasonic KX-P4455 PostScript laser.

Acknowledgements are due to Text 100 and Microsoft for Windows 3 and Word for Windows, Aldus for PageMaker, Rank Xerox for Ventura, and Panasonic for the printer.

Thanks are also due to the suppliers of the all applications mentioned in Part Five, Peter Dixon of Heinemann, Microsol for solving a problem, and Lorna.

INTRODUCTION

Introduction

Welcome, as they say, to the world of Windows. You can now say goodbye to the DOS prompt and 640 kilobyte memory restrictions. This book is concerned solely with Windows 3 and applications specifically developed for it, although many of the techniques covered are applicable to Windows 2, Windows 286 and Windows 386. Windows 3 is the latest version of Windows from Microsoft and was released in mid-1990. Within just a few months of the initial release its impact has been dramatic. What follows in this introduction is a discussion of strategies for the PC user, and the role Windows 3 plays in such strategies. Those readers who might not be interested in the DOS, DOS with Windows 3, OS/2, and UNIX debate can jump straight to Part One.

Most PC users have an operating system called DOS, and this has been the case for a number of years. The term DOS includes MSDOS, PCDOS and DRDOS. It makes little difference which one you have. MSDOS is the one you are most likely to possess and is the Microsoft product. PCDOS is the operating system supplied by IBM while DRDOS comes from Digital Research. DOS is rather boring and you cannot do a lot with it, unless you are a member of that esoteric bunch of DOS Masters. For most of us it puts the infamous prompt on screen (usually *A>* or *C>*) and the rest is up to you. If you know what you are doing you can change directories and run applications by keying in the program name. Invariably the applications you run are character-based or text-based, and make no or little use of graphics. As a group they are referred to as standard applications and include all the old favourites, Word-Perfect 5, dBase III+ and Lotus 1-2-3 release 2. Swapping data between such applications is not always that easy. Running two of them together is impossible unless you have Desqview,

Introduction

Windows 386 or Windows 3. Each application has its own peculiar set of commands and mode of working. Saving data to file, for example, requires F10 in WordPerfect, Ctrl-End in dBase and /,F,S in Lotus. Every time you buy a new package you have to plod through the whole arduous learning experience all over again. If that is not bad enough, the power, speed and features of the application are effectively limited by the inability of DOS to cope with large amounts of computer memory. Although various tricks can be employed to overcome this limit none of them have proved really satisfactory.

Until recently, therefore, PC history suggests DOS was becoming obsolete as an operating system for the PC. There are, fortunately, a number of alternatives around. People in the minicomputer and mainframe worlds have long been using an operating system called UNIX. This does not have the memory limitations of DOS and allows multi-tasking of applications. In other words you can switch from one application to another quickly – working in one while another is processing. Again historically, as the cost of memory and large hard disks fell, capabilities of the PC grew until it became feasible to install UNIX on a stand-alone machine. Perhaps the best known example is Santa Cruz Operation UNIX for the PC. This method began to emerge as a realistic way forward. Meanwhile Microsoft and IBM were developing a brand new operating system called OS/2, which was heralded by many as the answer. OS/2 overcomes the memory limit barrier and, like UNIX, is a multi-tasking operating system although it lacks the multi-user capabilities of UNIX.

Meanwhile, usually tucked away in the graphics and publishing departments of companies, a lucky minority were using a non-PC micro – the Apple Macintosh. What these fortunate few were using was a WIMP system. They pointed and clicked with a mouse, did not need to learn arcane command syntax, hardly touched the

Introduction

keyboard and found swapping data between applications a doddle. Their machines had little pictures on screen, called icons, and they found the software so easy to operate that manuals were left on the shelf. The word processor, spreadsheet and database they used all had a similar look and feel. Applications were 'intuitive', you could almost sense how they worked. There was only one learning curve, not myriad different ones for each and every application. Macintosh users, quite rightly, looked on the PC world with a mixture of disbelief and smugness. The acronym WIMP (windows, icons, mouse and pull-down menus) became a synonym for Apple. Software suppliers for PCs tried to learn from this approach. Digital Research brought out GEM and Microsoft released a package called Windows.

For one reason or another Windows, rather than GEM, gradually emerged as a more popular WIMP for the PC, though even it never really caught on. As it required DOS to be present it was still subject to the 640 kilobyte limit, it did not allow multi-tasking (apart from Windows 386), and the front end was not much friendlier than the old DOS prompt. You may have seen it around, as Windows 2.x, 286 or 386. Few applications emerged to exploit this new interface and it was notoriously slow. The acronym WIMP was replaced by GUI but it made little difference. People were putting their money on UNIX or OS/2. The latter had its own GUI (graphical user interface) and GUIs appeared for UNIX – Sun's Open Look and SCO's Open Desktop.

Despite all the criticism that earlier versions of Windows gave rise to, Microsoft and a couple of independent application developers kept faith. Windows was given a complete overhaul, PCs with plenty of memory dropped in price, and a host of independent software companies were convinced. The result is a GUI that seems to offer the best of all possible worlds – Windows 3 – first appearing around June 1990. It comes as something of a surprise,

Introduction

a pleasant surprise, for many users are familiar and at home with DOS – simply dreading starting all over again with OS/2 or UNIX.

Although Windows 3 sits on top of DOS it is no longer subject to the 640 kilobyte ceiling, thanks to some clever memory management. Thus if your computer has, say, 4 megabytes of RAM, you can exploit the full 4 megabytes. This, in turn, means you can multi-task and run more powerful programs more quickly. The front end is now a true GUI with icons rather than text. It is much faster than previous incarnations of Windows and within a couple of months of the launch there are literally hundreds of applications around that work in the Windows 3 environment. Like the Macintosh owner before, the PC user can choose a suite of applications that are intuitive, easy to learn and all with the same look and feel. It is simple to cut/copy and paste data between applications. Most applications support DDE (dynamic data exchange), which enables one application to send data and commands to another. Thus your database might open your spreadsheet, send it some data and instruct it to draw a chart. If the data in the database changes then this is reflected in the data and the chart in the spreadsheet.

Windows 3 has met with almost universal praise and has given DOS quite a few more years' life yet. Later in the book we'll take a look at some of the major applications available for Windows 3 and try to recommend a suite of applications for the normal business or home user. But do not worry if you do not have them yet, for Windows 3 will cope with not only Windows 2.x applications but also with standard DOS packages. There are even packages that allow you to run UNIX applications in Windows 3 on a DOS-based PC linked to a UNIX host.

If you have just bought Windows 3, or it was bundled with your PC, then you are not only going to enjoy using it but you have

Introduction

what appears to be the next industry standard for the PC. One projection I have seen, from a normally reliable and accurate analyst, suggests that as many as half of all PC owners will be using Windows 3 within two years. We shall have to wait and see.

PART ONE

Getting started

SECTION 1
Installing Windows 3

The installation and configuration of Windows 3 (from now on we'll refer to it as just Windows) is either simplicity itself or very complex and involved. If you have an IBM-compatible computer, an industry-standard mouse, a standard monitor, you're not on a network and you don't want to multi-task non-Windows applications, then all should be completely straightforward. Even if you are linked to a network and wish to run lots of non-Windows packages together, then installation should still proceed without a hitch; though you may have to fiddle with certain parameters after installation.

The Windows manual itself devotes a page-and-a-half to installation and contains only one main instruction. This is enough if you have some experience of your hardware. Remember you can press the F1 function key during installation to access Help. Instructions for installation are listed later. Even if you are totally new to computing you might like to try them now, in nine cases out of ten these instructions are sufficient. Should the installation fail in some way or you require more guidance, the brief list of instructions is followed by a rather more detailed breakdown of steps involved.

Before you start it is a good idea to make backup copies of the disks carrying your copy of Windows. One method of doing so is to type DISKCOPY A: A: (or DISKCOPY A: B:) at the DOS prompt and to press Enter.

To install Windows on your computer:

1 Place the Windows Disk 1 in the floppy disk drive. If you have two floppy disk drives place it in the first drive. You can, of course, use the second one, but you would then need to replace A: with B: in step 2.

■ SECTION 1
Installing Windows 3

2 Type **A:** and press the Enter key.

3 Type **SETUP** (the case is immaterial) and press the Enter key.

4 Follow the instructions that appear on screen and make the choices relevant to your machine. Pressing F1 summons the Setup program Help facility, should you be unsure about a particular instruction or choice.

If everything seems to proceed smoothly you can go straight to the section: Starting Windows. If the installation should fail – for example, your mouse does not work with Windows or you can not start Windows – then install it again, preferably by reading through the more detailed instructions later.

The next steps lead you through the installation routine once again, but this time with a detailed explanation of the instructions and choices.

1 Insert Windows Disk 1 in your floppy disk drive.

2 Type **A:** (or **B:**) and press the Enter key.

SECTION 1
Installing Windows 3

3 Type **SETUP** and press the Enter key. In a moment or two you will see the 'Welcome to Setup' screen. This informs you that the F1 function key accesses help with the installation, while F3 stops the whole procedure.

4 Press Enter to leave the first screen. The next screen is where you specify a directory on the hard disk in which to install Windows. In normal circumstances you would accept the default of C:\WINDOWS. You might want to alter this if you have a D: partition on the hard disk and C: has less than 6 megabytes free, in which case D:\WINDOWS might be a suitable alternative. If you have a copy of Windows 2 already installed on C:, in C:\WINDOWS, and you wish to keep it, then perhaps C:\WIN3 would be appropriate. Otherwise the default offered is fine.

5 Alter the default directory for Windows, if necessary, by using the Backspace and Delete keys. Press Enter to continue.

The subsequent display is the Setup routine's attempt to figure out the hardware you are using. Windows will usually guess correctly, although the type of mouse may not be right. If you are a European user then the keyboard layout and language have to be changed. This is due to the fact that Windows has no way of knowing which country it is in, and therefore presents the defaults of US for keyboard layout, and English (American) for language. If you have cause to amend any of the settings, place the highlight on the setting with the Up and Down arrow keys. Press Enter to see a list of alternatives. Pressing Esc backs you out of

SECTION 1
Installing Windows 3

this list leaving the initial setting intact. You can scroll down the list of alternatives with the Down arrow key. Pressing Enter when an alternative is highlighted causes that option to replace the initial setting. There is an entry for Other. Selecting this indicates your hardware configuration is not supported by Windows. In such a case you need to obtain a Windows driver from the hardware manufacturer, as Windows requires you to insert the floppy disk containing the driver in the floppy disk drive during installation. If you are in such a situation, and none of the more standard options have worked, you can not install Windows fully until you receive the driver from the manufacturer. If the driver needed is a simple mouse driver, however, you can get by in the meantime without a mouse by consulting the section: Essential Skills to discover keyboard alternatives to mouse actions. Fortunately in ninety nine percent of cases the drivers included with Windows are perfectly suitable.

Let us go through settings one by one. First parameter is labelled Computer. Your machine is probably MSDOS or PCDOS and this is presumably the default entry. This entry covers IBM and fully compatible machines. UK readers, in particular, might like to note that this is the option for Amstrad computers. A few machines are not part of this category, for example, some in the Hewlett-Packard range. If the installation fails, go back and see if your machine is on the list of alternatives. The second setting is Display. The defaults you can normally expect are Hercules, CGA, EGA, VGA, and VGA Monochrome. All of these are perfectly standard displays. There are other options for manufacturer-specific video display cards.

SECTION 1
Installing Windows 3

Mouse is the third setting, and this may cause problems. The default you can expect to see is, in all likelihood, Microsoft - IBM PS/2, Mouse Systems, or Logitech (serial or bus). Again UK readers should be aware that the Microsoft - IBM PS/2 option works with the Amstrad mouse (unless you happen to have an early version of the PC2386 – in which case you should contact Amstrad or your dealer for the correct driver).

There are various reasons why the cause of trouble is often the mouse. Many mice are not truly compatible with those featured in the list. On some machines either the serial or the bus port are not configured correctly. This can often be solved by re-setting switches inside the computer. Your computer supplier should be able to give advice on this. But the usual culprit is frequently the DOS mouse driver. If this is already loaded it may conflict with the Windows mouse driver, resulting in failure of the latter. The DOS mouse driver often lurks in the DOS directory and is called MOUSE.COM or MOUSE.SYS. It is loaded by typing MOUSE at the DOS prompt or something like DEVICE=MOUSE.SYS. On many computers the mouse is set up automatically by a line in the AUTOEXEC.BAT file. Any line containing MOUSE should be removed from that file for the mouse to work properly with Windows. Refer to your computer manual or contact your dealer if you do not know how to edit a text file. You might be able to soldier on without a mouse and later consult the exercises on Notepad in Part Two. Notepad is the Windows text editor and can be used to edit your AUTOEXEC.BAT.

Next parameter to look at is Keyboard. If you have twelve function keys across the top of the keyboard, you can expect to see the default Enhanced 101 or 102 Key US or Non US

■ SECTION 1
Installing Windows 3

Keyboard. If you have ten function keys the option for 84 keys should be showing. The fifth setting is Keyboard Layout. Unless you are a US reader or need to maintain strict compatibility with US colleagues this should be changed. UK users should alter the default US setting to British. The next selection, entitled Language, is very similar. The default is English (American). UK readers will find English (International) more appropriate.

The final setting is Network. The likely default is Not installed, Novell, Vines, 3Com or LAN Manager. If Windows guesses wrongly then change it. It is important to note that this setting, as indeed many of the others, can be altered after you have installed the software, by selecting the Windows Setup icon. Sometimes, however, the wrong setting for Mouse or Display prevents installation and you have no choice but to go through the whole installation routine again. A short cut to save going back to scratch, worth investigating, is to change to your Windows directory on the hard disk, type SETUP and press Enter.

6 When you are completely satisfied with the settings, highlight the No changes setting which should be reading *The above list matches my computer.* Press Enter.

The Setup routine starts to copy the relevant files from your Windows disks. You are prompted to change disks from time to time. After you have done so, click OK (assuming your mouse works) or press Enter. During copying of files from Windows Disk 2 the screen changes from text mode to graphics mode. You will notice the first of the Windows buttons and hopefully a mouse pointer that moves with the mouse. If the pointer does not move you have the incorrect

SECTION 1
Installing Windows 3

mouse driver (or your mouse ports need configuring, or the DOS mouse driver is loaded). It is usually possible to continue installation with the keyboard and to alter the mouse driver later. This is accomplished through the Windows Setup icon that you will see after Windows is started. Occasionally the wrong mouse driver causes Windows to crash. If this is so try changing to the WINDOWS directory on the hard disk then, at the DOS prompt, type SETUP and press Enter. This enables you to alter the mouse driver without going through all the installation routine again. Otherwise you will have to repeat the whole installation from the beginning.

This first graphics screen has a couple of reminders at the bottom. F1 gets help and F3 aborts installation. (Pressing F3, at any time, means that Windows will either not work at all or at best only partially.) A moveable mouse pointer should be visible on screen. In addition there are three check boxes. Check boxes enable you to turn selections on or off – a cross in the box indicating selection. The three check boxes are for Set up Printers, Set up Applications Already on Hard Disk, and Read on line Documents. It is not necessary to choose any of these. They can all be carried out later if you wish, and will not affect whether Windows starts up or not. To turn a check box on or off you click with the mouse. If you have no mouse or your mouse is not working at this stage, move to the check box with the Tab key and change the setting with the Spacebar. Should you experience any difficulty with the keyboard alternatives to the mouse during installation, refer to the section: Essential Skills. I normally advise people to choose Set up Printers and Set up Applications. Reading the on line Documents might be confusing for someone new to computing.

■ SECTION 1
Installing Windows 3

7 When the check boxes are how you want them click the OK button. For those of you without a mouse simply press Enter instead.

Setup then spends a few minutes copying files from the Windows disks to your hard disk. You will be kept informed of which programs and fonts are being copied. You will be asked to insert disks from time to time. Make sure that the drive letter is the appropriate one, A: or B:. After inserting the disk click OK or press Enter. When the fonts have been copied Setup builds the front end for Windows, which is called Program Manager. This is basically a menu system that allows you to start applications and utilities easily. Program Manager subsidiary (or document) windows are also constructed. These will have the names Main, Accessories and Games.

8 Once all of this is completed you are asked if you want Setup to modify your AUTOEXEC.BAT and CONFIG.SYS files. Unless you are familiar with DOS path names and how to load SYS files it is best to let Setup carry on. Original AUTOEXEC.BAT and CONFIG.SYS files are not lost, instead they are automatically renamed AUTOEXEC.OLD and CONFIG.OLD. If for any reason you decide not to use Windows on a regular basis, you could rename the new files AUTOEXEC.WIN and CONFIG.WIN, and rename the OLD files back to AUTOEXEC.BAT and CONFIG.SYS. Whenever you change your AUTOEXEC.BAT or CONFIG.SYS it is essential that you reboot the computer for them to take effect.

Unless you have a good reason not to, leave the option (radio) button highlighted for Setup to modify the

SECTION 1
Installing Windows 3

AUTOEXEC.BAT and CONFIG.SYS files. To choose one of the other options instead you simply click its option button. Use the arrow (direction) keys if you do not have a mouse. Click Continue or press Enter to move on.

9 Next stage involves letting Windows know about your printer or printers. This is done through the Printer dialogue which should now be on screen. If you do not possess a printer or wish to define the printers later, by using Windows Control Panel, simply click OK or press Enter. If you are new to Windows and have a printer it is probably a good idea to choose a printer at this point. Doing so means that you will be able to print immediately, once Windows is installed. To install a printer make sure the check box Print Manager is selected, which is the default. The Print Manager allows you to spool and control printing in the background and is discussed in detail later in the book.

There are two main list boxes in the dialogue. The top one is empty and this is where the chosen printer will be listed. The lower one contains available printers. You can scroll through this list by clicking up and down arrows on the vertical scroll bar. Pressing Page Up or Page Down keys jumps quickly through the list.

0 Find your printer in the list of available printers. If your printer is not listed find one which is compatible. You may have to consult your printer manual to discover compatible printers.

■ SECTION 1
Installing Windows 3

In the rare event that your printer or a compatible printer is not shown in the list you should try choosing the Generic / Text Only option and ask your dealer for a Windows 3 driver for your particular printer. While you are waiting for the driver to arrive you should be able to print text, albeit of suspect quality. The driver for your printer can be installed later through Control Panel by choosing Unlisted Printer.

11 Select the relevant printer by clicking its name then click the Install button. From the keyboard use the direction keys and press Enter. Setup will ask you to insert one of the Windows disks. Do so and click OK, or press Enter.

The name of the printer appears in the top list of installed printers. There are one or two other things that Windows needs to know about your printer. You must specify the port to which your printer is attached, usually LPT1 which is the main parallel port. And depending on your particular printer, you can set such parameters as paper size, printing resolution and page orientation. If you are in any doubt over the parameters you can try US Letter or A4 for paper size, the highest resolution for printing, and portrait orientation for the page. Laser printers have more options, for example for font cartridges. Your dealer may be able to give advice if you are unsure of the correct choices. Windows also asks for something called Timeouts. Accept the defaults presented when this happens.

12 With the name of the installed printer highlighted in the list box at the top of the dialogue click the Configure button to

SECTION 1
Installing Windows 3

see the Printer Configure dialogue. If you are not using the mouse you can move around the dialogue with the Tab key, move within sections of a dialogue with the direction keys, and press Enter to carry out commands. Highlight the relevant port for your printer and accept the Timeouts defaults by clicking Setup.

3 Next dialogue differs from printer to printer. The title of the dialogue reflects the printer currently being configured and is where you set paper size and so on. It is impossible to give much guidance here as the settings depend upon the individual user and printer. Make the choices that seem appropriate or accept the defaults.

You will see a list box called Printer. This is actually a pull-down list and is accessed by clicking the down arrow to the right. Keyboard users need to press the Down arrow key while holding down the Alt key. This pull-down list allows you to specify more exactly the type of printer and is worth investigating. Click OK, or press Enter, when you are satisfied with your settings.

You are now returned to the Printers Configure dialogue.

4 Click OK, or press Enter, in the Printers Configure dialogue.

You can repeat steps 10 to 14 for additional printers should you wish. The final stage in configuring a printer is to check it is the active printer. This is only necessary if you install more than one printer.

■ SECTION 1
Installing Windows 3

15 If you have more than one printer in the list of installed printers at the top of the Printers dialogue, highlight your main printer and click the Active option button. From the keyboard you may have to tab to the correct section first and turn on the appropriate option button with the direction keys.

16 Whether you chose one or more printers click OK, or press Enter, to exit the printer installation routine.

17 Last part of Windows Setup involves picking those applications you would like to see depicted in Windows. This means the application, whether Windows-based or not, can be run simply by clicking its icon (you can also use a keyboard alternative). Once again it is possible to pick applications at a later date, though, until you are familiar with Windows Program Manager, I would advise you to pick the applications now. This is done with the Set Up Applications dialogue. Before you see this dialogue you must tell Setup where to look for applications. You do this in the dialogue currently on screen. Unless you have good reason not to, let Setup search all drives. This means that drives C and D, for example, are searched if you have two partitions on your hard disk.

Click the down arrow (or press the Alt and Down arrow keys together) to see search options and highlight the appropriate choice. Click OK, or press Enter, to summon the Set Up Applications dialogue. The dialogue presents a list of all the major applications it finds on its search path.

SECTION 1
Installing Windows 3

8 If you are happy with the contents of the list click the Add All button (on the keyboard this is Alt-A) to accept all the contents.

These are copied to the empty list box on the right. Should you prefer you can click items one by one and click Add. Items may always be deselected by clicking Remove. You might prefer this method of individual selection if Setup finds some unexpected and unrequired applications on your hard disk. Occasionally, say, there might be two or more entries for the same application! This occurs when Setup detects help programs and applications that are part of larger applications. Normally you would want to choose the main application only. Help programs are usually run from within the main program and not as separate stand-alone applications.

9 Click OK, or press Enter, when the right-hand list details the correct entries.

10 Remove any disk in the floppy disk drive and click the Reboot button, or press Enter, to finish installation of Windows and restart the computer. The latter is vitally important as you presumably allowed Windows to alter the AUTOEXEC.BAT and CONFIG.SYS files which only take effect on booting up.

You will soon find out if all has gone well when you move to the next section.

SECTION 2
Starting Windows

It is possible that you have read articles or heard people referring to Windows operating modes. These should not be the cause for any concern, except in one eventuality. Thus you can ignore any discussion of switches and their purpose until you are comfortable with Windows and running applications from Windows. Switches are the extra parameters specified when you start Windows. The exception mentioned is discussed shortly and involves forcing Windows to start in real mode.

■   To start Windows normally simply type **WIN** at the DOS prompt.

After a second or two you see the Windows 3 logo which is replaced by the Program Manager window. It will say Program Manager in its title bar. If the computer jumps back to the DOS prompt or hangs completely before Program Manager shows, go back through the section on installation. This also applies if you do see Program Manager but moving the mouse fails to move the mouse pointer across the screen.

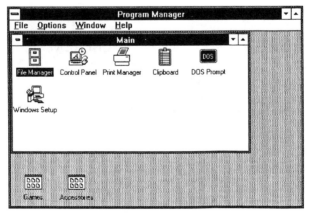

Windows initial screen

SECTION 2
Starting Windows

As your confidence in Windows grows you will find that you never have to revert to the DOS prompt. As well as being able to run all your applications from Windows, you will increasingly use Windows for all your file and disk management. In such a situation it seems a shame to have to type the initial WIN command at the DOS prompt. You can eliminate even this step by adding the line WIN to the AUTOEXEC.BAT file in the root directory. For now you might find it more convenient to add the line using your usual text editor (EDLIN or RPED, for example) or with your favourite word processor. The latter course necessitates loading and saving the file in ASCII format. Ultimately you will find it much easier to use Notepad, the Windows text editor. Having done so, the next time you turn on the computer or reboot, Windows will start automatically. Hopefully you will never see the DOS prompt again, except fleetingly as you quit Windows in order to switch off.

For that very tiny minority of readers who can still not get Windows running or it works only very slowly or it hangs – after checking through the detailed installation instructions in this book – try some of the following. (If you are a newcomer to computing you would do well to seek assistance in working through this list of tips).

■ Look at your AUTOEXEC.BAT and CONFIG.SYS files. These contain various settings any of which, if incorrect, may be the cause of problems. FILES should be about 30; BUFFERS 20, or 10 with SMARTDRV; memory resident programs should preferably not be loaded; HIMEM.SYS should be there if you have extended memory; SMARTDRV.SYS is advisable (note that Setup would have made the relevant entries for HIMEM and SMARTDRV for you, if you allowed it to configure your files during installation); depending on your hardware and version of DOS then STACKS, SHARE and APPEND may cause problems.

SECTION 2
Starting Windows

- These and other points are covered in the Windows User's Guide. Consult the guide, in particular chapter 13 (Optimizing Windows) and Appendix D (Command Lines in the CONFIG.SYS File). Some of the issues, especially those covering expanded memory, can be a shade technical. You are recommended to consult your dealer or a colleague experienced in Windows 3.

- There is often a simple adjustment to be made. Many of these are documented in the TXT files that Setup copies to your Windows directory. These are text files and can be viewed in and printed from your normal text editor or your favourite word processor.

- If you plan to run non-Windows applications from Windows and have an EGA monitor then you must add the line DEVICE=C:\WINDOWS\EGA.SYS to your CONFIG.SYS. Replace WINDOWS in this command line with the name of the Windows directory, should yours be different.

All users would do well to create a new directory to store temporary Windows files and add SET TEMP=C:\directory name to the AUTOEXEC.BAT file. Many Windows operations create temporary files which in normal circumstances are automatically deleted. Sometimes, however, the files are not deleted, usually when the application hangs, and they clutter up the directory. The SET TEMP command keeps them tidily in the specified directory – not in the root directory. From time to time they can be deleted if they begin to eat up disk space. Never delete such files while still in Windows – this is about the only time you will see the DOS prompt!

When it starts up, Windows checks your system and invokes the appropriate operating mode. There are three modes; real, standard and enhanced (386) mode. Broadly speaking these three

SECTION 2
Starting Windows

modes are for 8086, 80286 and 80386/486 computers respectively, although amount of memory in your computer has an effect too. Windows knows which mode to choose for your computer. To check the operating mode click Help in the Program Manager window then About Program Manager in the pull-down menu. The message invoked indicates current mode. Click OK to remove the message. Keyboard users should press Alt-H (press H while holding down the Alt key), then press A, and press Enter to remove the message. Many instructions in this book, from this point on, are for the mouse. Keyboard users are recommended to study the section: Essential Skills for keyboard alternatives.

I mentioned earlier that you need not worry about operating modes, with one exception. If you plan to run older Windows applications (those before Windows 3) and the current mode is standard or enhanced then you will have to force Windows to start in real mode. Trying to run such an application, by clicking its icon in Program Manager, displays a message advising you to run in real mode. In such a case quit Windows (see the section: Quitting Windows) and restart in real mode. To force Windows into real mode type WIN/R at the DOS prompt.

Real mode is not as powerful as standard or enhanced mode. If default mode is standard or enhanced then you are not using all your computer's resources by forcing real mode. In this situation it is worth considering replacement of your old Windows applications with versions specifically created for use with Windows 3. Many software suppliers have special deals allowing you to upgrade reasonably cheaply. You are strongly advised to take advantage of such offers before they are phased out. In Part Five there is a discussion of major applications and version numbers available for Windows 3. If default mode on your machine is real mode then you do not have to worry about older Windows applications.

■ SECTION 3
Printing from Windows

Provided you specified one or more printers during Setup then printing should present few problems. Printing from Windows and from Windows-based applications is normally carried out by clicking File then Print (though you will not see this in Program Manager itself). Standard applications, for example WordPerfect 5.1, when run from Windows, print in their usual way. The section: Control Panel includes a second look at installing printers. If your printer fails to work you should refer to that section.

■ SECTION 4
Quitting Windows

There are numerous ways of closing Windows. The methods available are normally available with all Windows-based applications too. Experiment until you find the method which feels the most comfortable.

To quit Windows with a mouse:

1 Click the Control menu to access a pull-down menu. The Control menu is at the very top left of the Program Manager, just above the File menu option and to the left of the title bar. It contains a small symbol which represents a spacebar. (Some documentation may refer to the Control menu as the System menu).

2 In the pull-down menu click Close. The Exit Windows dialogue appears.

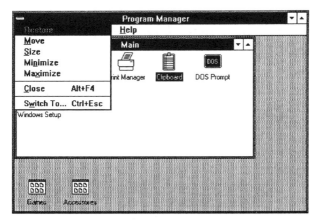

Control menu

■ SECTION 4
Quitting Windows

3 Make sure the Save Changes check box in this dialogue is empty. Click the check box to remove any check mark. This box should be checked only if you have changed the Program Manager layout and wish to preserve the changes you have made. If it is empty then Windows will forget the changes and revert to the former layout. We are assuming that you have not made any changes which you consider worth keeping yet.

4 Click OK to return to the DOS prompt. If this is the end of a session then you are now in a position to park the hard disk heads (if that is part of your normal procedure) and to switch the computer off.

Steps 1 and 2 can be replaced by simply double clicking the Control menu. This for most people is the preferred method of leaving Windows. Another alternative is to use the File menu. To quit with the File menu:

1 Click File then Exit Windows in the subsequent pull-down menu.

2 See steps 3 and 4 earlier.

To quit Windows with the keyboard:

1 Press Alt-Spacebar to access the Control pull-down menu.

■ SECTION 4
Quitting Windows

2 Press C for Close, or use the Down arrow key to highlight Close and press Enter.

3 See steps 3 and 4 earlier. The Save Changes check box can be altered from the keyboard too: press Tab to highlight the option (a small dotted rectangle surrounds the box title) and press Spacebar to add or remove the check mark.

If you prefer to use the File menu then:

1 Press Alt-F and then press X for Exit Windows. Instead of pressing X you could highlight Exit Windows with the Down arrow key and press Enter.

2 See step 3 immediately preceding.

There is also what is called a keyboard shortcut. This involves pressing Alt-F4, that is: press the F4 function key while holding down the Alt key.

If you had started any applications and had not closed them down Windows alerts you to the fact that applications are still running. You would then save your work, return to the application, or leave the application without saving your work.

SECTION 5
Essential skills

Windows adopts certain conventions and they have to be learnt in order to get anywhere. If you are new to computing, or have never used a GUI before then some of the skills may seem a little bizarre at first, but it is all certainly worthwhile. If you are using a mouse for the first time please rest assured that after a couple of days you will not even notice that it is there, it all becomes totally automatic. You will find that the mouse is eventually very much easier (and quicker) to use than the keyboard. Whether you have a mouse or not you will discover that the techniques learnt here apply to all Windows-based applications. So if you detect any steepness in the learning curve it helps to remember subsequent learning curves for applications and accessories are relatively flat. Windows itself and Windows-based applications have a similar look and feel. Working through the essential skills will make the transition from the game Solitaire (we'll play this shortly – UK readers probably know the game as Patience) to a powerful application like Superbase (a Windows database which you buy separately) so much simpler.

Readers without a mouse are strongly encouraged to get one (make sure it is supported by Windows – for example a Microsoft, Logitech or Mouse Systems compatible mouse). You will not regret it. In the meantime you should note that the practical exercises in this book are documented for the mouse only. Everything in the book is actually possible via the keyboard, though for some of the heavy-weight Windows applications a mouse provides the only real practical method for some actions. You should experience no disadvantage when working through the exercises here, for the essential skills cover all the standard keyboard alternatives. By later concentrating on mouse actions we can cover more in the limited space of this book than would otherwise have been possible with two sets of instructions. It also makes the book that much easier to read and, besides, most people who have bought Windows 3 already have a mouse.

SECTION 5
Essential skills

Readers familiar with earlier versions of Windows are also advised to work through the essential skills. Windows 3 includes a number of conventions, terms and features that are completely new.

The initial screen

Once Windows has started it displays the initial screen. If you have had Windows installed for a while then your initial screen may be quite a bit different from the example screen-shot shown. You will need to adapt the exercises to match your display. In any case if you have altered the default start up screen, you probably know what you are doing anyway! Incidentally the screen-shot was captured in Windows itself by using Clipboard. Even if you have not used Windows yet, then some of the elements of the window may be slightly different. What you should see is a window called Program Manager, containing a smaller window entitled Main. Underneath this second window, but still within the first window, you will notice some small rectangles. These are named

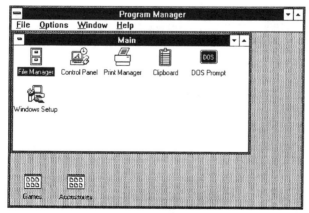

Windows initial screen

SECTION 5
Essential skills

Accessories and Games. In addition, and depending upon your particular computer, you might see rectangles for Windows Applications and Non-Windows Applications. These rectangles are windows too, albeit very small ones. When a window is shrunk to its smallest possible size it does not look much like an ordinary window, and is known as an icon.

Components of a window

All windows look more or less identical. This applies to Windows itself and Windows-based applications. A window is merely an area on screen that has distinct boundaries. A window may be as large as the screen, shrunk to an icon, or any size between. It is possible to have two or more windows showing at once. If you refer to your initial screen you will notice that there are two windows, one inside the other. There are also some smaller windows in the form of icons. On your display you might have two, three or four of these icons. The two windows are called Program Manager and Main. If we take a trip around the Program Manager window we

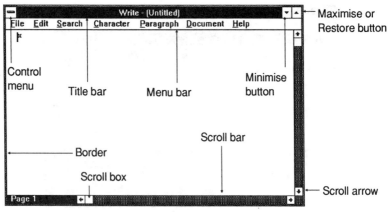

A typical window

SECTION 5
Essential skills

can identify its features. At the top left of the window is the Control menu box. Clicking this pulls down a menu. To remove the menu you click once anywhere outside the menu. This menu appears in most windows and is used to carry out a variety of tasks. To the right of this is the title bar. This contains the name of the window and in applications indicates the name of the data file on which you are working. In an inactive window the title bar is white, in an active window it is coloured or more intense. At the top right are two buttons. The one on the left contains a downward pointing arrowhead and is called the Minimise button. The next one contains an upward pointing arrowhead and is the Maximise button. Do not worry if you sometimes notice two arrowheads on this button. Above this top row of Control menu, title bar, Minimise and Maximise buttons is a thin band. The band extends around the whole perimeter of the window and is called the border. At each corner of the window the border is partitioned by two small lines. This area of the border is referred to as a window corner. Beneath the top row of the window is a second row containing the words File, Options, Window and Help. These are all used to access pull-down (or drop-down menus) and the row is called the menu bar. The area of the window enclosed by the menu bar and the left, right, and bottom border is the workspace. Some windows have extra features like scroll bars, but they are not shown for the Program Manager window.

The second window, Main, is very similar in structure to the Program Manager window, except it does not have a menu bar. Windows with menu bars are application windows, those without are document windows.

Icons

Icons are minimised windows. There are two major categories of icons. Application icons are used to start (or restore) application

SECTION 5
Essential skills

windows. Document icons are for opening document windows. In the Main window the icon labelled File Manager is an application icon while the icon at the bottom of the Program Manager window, labelled Accessories, is a document icon. There are in fact two varieties of application icons: the Windows manual makes this distinction and you may see references to program item icons.

Mouse actions

There are five mouse actions normally carried out while working with Windows and Windows-based applications. Four are used all the time and the fifth, known as right clicking is used only rarely. The other four are referred to as moving, clicking, double clicking and dragging. It is important to keep practicing these actions until you feel quite comfortable with the mouse. Many people take to the mouse straight away, a minority requires that extra bit of patience.

Make sure you have an area of your desktop free to manoeuvre the mouse. To begin with have as large an area as possible to the right or in front of the keyboard, at least a square foot. As you become more proficient you should find this area can be as small as about six inches by four inches. Always work with the mouse tail pointing away from you, towards the top of the desk. Rest your right hand gently on the mouse with the index finger lightly on the left hand mouse button. Of course the left-handed reader should reverse these positions. The difficulty here arises because your index finger is naturally on the right hand button. You really need to have your index finger on the left hand button because first, the index finger is the most natural finger to use for clicking and second, the left hand button is pressed most of the time. The solution is to swap functions of left and right mouse buttons. This can be accomplished by configuring the mouse through the Control Panel (see the entry on Mouse in the section on Control

SECTION 5
Essential skills

Panel). Should your mouse have three buttons you can ignore the middle button.

Moving the mouse across the desktop results in a corresponding movement of mouse pointer on screen. Try to move the mouse with your hand still resting on top and your thumb and little (or second finger) lightly gripping the flanks of the mouse. Do not move the mouse by holding it between your thumb and index finger in a pincer fashion. A small amount of downward pressure may be necessary. Any failure of the pointer to keep track with the mouse indicates an unsuitable surface for the mouse. Some laminated desk tops are just too smooth, and a sheet of coarse paper under the mouse will help. Better still is a mouse mat. You may discover that you run out of room on your desk before the mouse reaches the edges of the screen. Just pick up the mouse and place it in a more central position. Picking up the mouse has no effect on its pointer location.

Clicking, or single clicking, is the action of pressing the left button once and letting it go quickly. Depending upon make of mouse there should ideally be a single audible click and possibly some tactile feedback as the button is pressed. It is important not to push the mouse away as you press the button, this may give unexpected and undesired results.

Double clicking is simply single clicking twice rapidly. Beginners often double click either too quickly or too slowly, and a few people can never quite manage it comfortably. Once again it is essential that you keep the mouse totally still as you double click. You can adjust the speed required for double clicking through Control Panel.

Dragging the mouse requires that you press and hold down the left hand mouse button, during which time you move the mouse

■ SECTION 5
Essential skills

across the desk top. It is better here to keep the button down until you are entirely satisfied with the location of the pointer. Your action has no effect until you let go of the button. Letting go too soon might have surprising results.

Right clicking which is only occasionally used signifies pressing the right hand button with the middle finger and immediately letting go. You may have reason to right click in Paintbrush to alter background colours, or in PageMaker and Superbase (the latter two are separate applications and are not included in Windows).

Other mouse techniques you might come across are right dragging, right double clicking, shift and control clicking. However to begin productive work it is sufficient to be able to move, click, double click and drag the mouse. Keyboard users should note that there are alternatives to these actions that do not require the mouse.

Mouse and keyboard practice

If you are new to Windows and mouse, it is vital to practice basic mouse actions in this section. If you are new to Windows and do not have a mouse you need to understand keyboard alternatives that follow each step below.

1 Move the mouse until the tip of the pointer is over the word File in the menu bar of the Program Manager window. Practice will show how accurate you must be, there is some degree of leeway allowed in positioning the pointer.

■ SECTION 5
Essential skills

2 Click the mouse and a pull-down menu appears. To make a choice from the menu you click the choice. For now we will back out of the action.

Keyboard alternative – Press Alt-F. The Alt key with the letter in a menu option is the standard procedure for accessing the menu.

3 Click anywhere apart from the menu to remove it. You might find it convenient merely to click File again.

Keyboard alternative – Press Esc. The word File will be highlighted. Pressing Esc a second time removes the highlight.

4 Double click the Control menu. If you are successful in double clicking the Exit Windows dialogue appears. Click

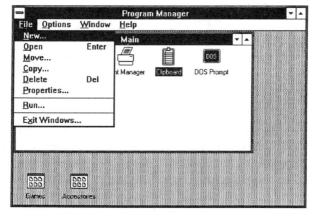

File menu

47

SECTION 5
Essential skills

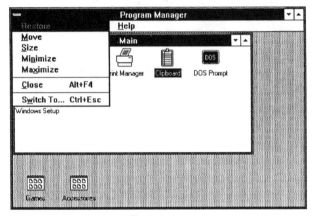

Control menu

Cancel to back out of your action. If you did not double click fast enough, or indeed too rapidly, Windows will interpret your action as a single click and display a pull-down menu. Should this happen click anywhere outside this pull-down menu to remove it and try again. Clicking in the original position also removes the menu.

Keyboard alternative – Press Alt-Spacebar then C then Esc. Pressing C chooses Close. You do not use Alt-letter within menus, only to access menus. Instead of pressing C you could move to Close with the direction keys and press Enter.

It is possible a slow double click combined with an unwanted movement of the mouse causes unexpected things to happen. You might see a dialogue box pop up on screen, or a four headed arrow, or Program Manager leaps to fill the screen, or even seems to disappear altogether. What has occurred is that Windows has interpreted the slow double click to be two quite distinct single clicks. The first single

SECTION 5
Essential skills

click opened the menu, the involuntary movement of the mouse positioned the pointer over a menu option and the second single click chose the option. To get rid of any dialogue box, click the Cancel button in the dialogue box. If you have summoned a four headed arrow, click anywhere on screen to restore the normal mouse pointer. A larger than normal Program Manager means an inadvertent choice of maximising. In this case locate the up and down arrow heads on the button at the extreme top right of the screen and click this button. This is actually the maximise button, which changes to being a restore button whenever a window is maximised. A disappearing Program Manager suggests an accidental minimising, it will be an icon at the bottom of the screen. To restore the icon to a window double click the icon. The fact that you are in this situation is a result of faulty double clicking. It is possible that your second attempt at double clicking does not work either. Should you now see a menu that has popped up from the icon click Restore in the menu. If nothing at all happens, first click the icon then click Restore in the resulting menu. Go back to step 4 until you get it working.

5 Click the maximise button on the Program Manager window (not the Main window). Program Manager expands to fill the whole display and the maximise button has changed slightly - there is an extra arrowhead. It is now a restore button.

Keyboard alternative – Press Alt-Spacebar then X. Such a sequence of keystrokes is represented by Alt-Spacebar, X from here on.

SECTION 5
Essential skills

6 Click the restore button to revert to the original size of Program Manager.

Keyboard alternative – Alt-Spacebar, R.

7 Click the minimise button to shrink the window to an icon. Note the Main window goes. This is because Main is a subsidiary document window within the Program Manager window.

Keyboard alternative – Alt-Spacebar, N.

8 Move the mouse pointer to the Program Manager icon and drag the mouse. The icon moves with the mouse across the screen. Stop dragging the mouse to anchor the icon in its new position.

Program Manager minimised

■ SECTION 5
Essential skills

Keyboard alternative – Alt-Spacebar, M. Then use the direction keys and press Enter to anchor the icon in position.

9 Drag the icon back to approximately its original position.

Keyboard alternative – Repeat the actions for step 8.

10 Double click the icon to restore the window. Note the Main window is back inside the Program Manager window. If you are experiencing problems with double clicking try single clicking the icon, and clicking Restore in the ensuing menu.

Keyboard alternative – Alt-Spacebar, R.

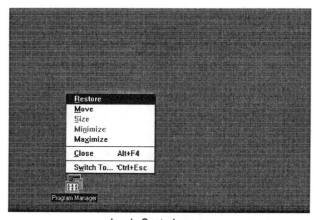

Icon's Control menu

■ SECTION 5
Essential skills

11 Click the minimise button in the Main window (not Program Manager this time). The Main window becomes a document icon in the Program Manager window.

Keyboard alternative – Alt-Hyphen, N. Note that Alt-Spacebar accesses the Control Menu in application windows, Alt-Hyphen is used in document windows.

12 Double click the Games document icon. Or try clicking and choosing Restore. There is now a document window for Games. Inside there are two application icons for Solitaire (Patience) and Reversi (Othello).

Keyboard alternative – Alt-W, 1. Alt-W pulls down the Windows menu. Each document icon and window has an associated underlined number. It is possible that Games is not number 1, in which case press the relevant number key.

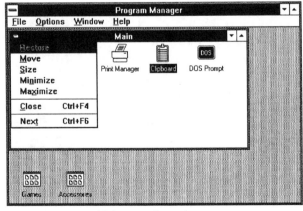

Main group Control menu

SECTION 5
Essential skills

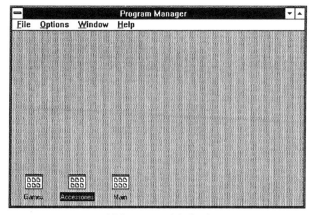

Main group minimised

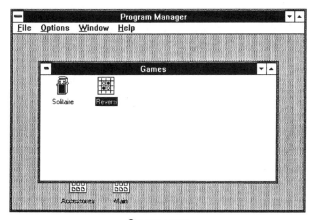

Games group

SECTION 5
Essential skills

13 Double click the Solitaire icon and take a break. Or single click to highlight the name Solitaire and press Enter.

Keyboard alternative – Use direction keys to move between application icons in the Games window. When Solitaire is highlighted press Enter. Solitaire is much easier to play if you have a mouse, though you can move cards with the keyboard. Experiment with tab and direction keys, and the spacebar. You can always press Alt-H, K which summons a help screen for keyboard users. Use Alt-Spacebar, C to remove the help screen. Alt-H, K is available in many accessories and applications to provide guidance to keyboard users.

14 When you have finally won at Solitaire double click its Control menu to close it down, back to an application icon.

Keyboard alternative – Alt-Spacebar, C.

Indiscriminate clicking may have minimised Solitaire to an icon beneath Program Manager. You may well be staring at two identical icons for Solitaire. The one in the Games window starts the application. The one at the foot of the screen represents a program already started and still running. You can close it down by double clicking the icon. Such icons retain any data present in the application. Minimising applications in this manner is a good way of tidying up the screen without recourse to saving data and closing applications. Should you see a pack of Solitaire icons (a pack of packs of cards, so to speak) at the bottom of the display you have started Solitaire more than once. Close each occurrence of the program by double clicking its icon – though not the one in the Games window, this only starts up more games.

SECTION 5
Essential skills

5 Minimise the Games window with its minimise button.

Keyboard alternative – Alt-Hyphen, N.

6 Open the Accessories window by double clicking its document icon. Remember you can click and press Enter if you prefer.

Keyboard alternative – Alt-W, 5. Check that 5 is the number next to Accessories in the Window pull-down menu. Your number could well be different.

In the Accessories window there are quite a few applications icons. You start these just the same as for Solitaire. Indeed if you have other document icons labelled Windows Applications and Non-Windows Applications, you open these by double clicking and start any programs they contain by double clicking the

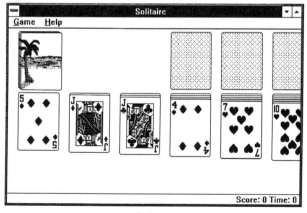

Solitaire

55

■ SECTION 5
Essential skills

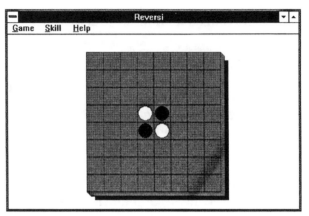

Reversi

relevant application icons. It is quite possible that your Program Manager does not include one or both of these windows. The Windows Applications group (document windows and icons within Program Manager are called groups) is created by Setup only if it discovers Windows-based applications on your hard disk. The Non-Windows Applications group will contain any standard DOS-based applications.

17 Double click the icon for Paintbrush in the Accessories window. Unnecessary movement of the mouse at this point could well dislodge the icon from its original position. This shifting of icons results in untidy group windows and you could eventually lose icons past the edge of the window. Of course you can easily get them back, but for now I recommend you reposition dislodged icons by dragging them back into place.

SECTION 5
Essential skills

Keyboard alternative – Use direction keys to move to Paintbrush and press Enter.

Paintbrush opens in its own window and partly, or completely, obscures the Program Manager window which now lies underneath.

8 Minimise Paintbrush by clicking the minimise button in the Paintbrush window.

Keyboard alternative – Alt-Spacebar, N.

9 In the Accessories group window in the Program Manager window double click the icon for Notepad.

Keyboard alternative – Use the direction keys to move to Notepad and press Enter.

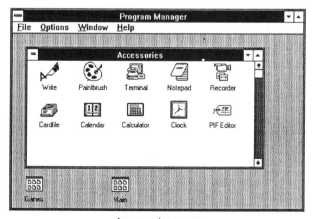

Accessories group

■ SECTION 5
Essential skills

20 Minimise Notepad too.

Keyboard alternative – Alt-Spacebar, N.

21 Minimise Program Manager itself, be careful to use the minimise button for Program Manager and not for the Accessories window.

Keyboard alternative – Alt-Spacebar, N.

You should now see three icons at the foot of the display. Paintbrush and Notepad are actually running applications, and the icons contain any work you carried out in those applications. This is one of the many ways of working with multiple applications in Windows. As you temporarily finish one application you minimise it, and begin work on another application. When you wish

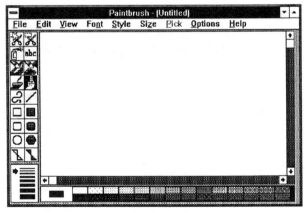

Paintbrush

SECTION 5
Essential skills

to return to the first application you minimise the current application and restore the first by double clicking its icon.

2 Restore Program Manager, Paintbrush and Notepad by double clicking their respective icons.

Keyboard alternative – Press Alt-Tab until the Program Manager icon is highlighted and let go of both keys. Repeat Alt-Tab for Paintbrush and Notepad.

You might find that opening an icon results in a large window which hides remaining icons from view. Then it is impossible to double click a chosen icon. In this event press the Tab key while holding down the Alt key until you see the title of the icon at the bottom of the screen and let go of both keys.

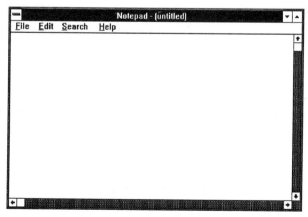

Notepad

■ SECTION 5
Essential skills

23 The Notepad window should be at the front. Do not worry if you restored the applications in a different order from here, all we are going to do is to maximise all the applications. Maximise Notepad or the front window.

Keyboard alternative – Alt-Spacebar, X.

The other two windows disappear behind the maximised window. We want to bring them to the front, in other words to make them current windows. Following actions are very important and fundamental to working with multiple applications. They involve switching the current application when some or all the other applications are in hidden windows. There are various methods of doing this and you will need to experiment until you discover the one that suits you. Some involve combination key strokes – Ctrl-Esc, Alt-Tab and Alt-Esc. If part of a hidden window is visible then clicking the visible portion brings that window to the front.

24 Press Esc while holding down the Ctrl key (if your keyboard has two Ctrl keys then either will do). You could click the Control menu followed by the Switch To option instead.

Keyboard alternative – Ctrl-Esc.

The Ctrl-Esc combinations summons the small Task List window. In the list box in this window you will see the currently open applications: Program Manager, Paintbrush and Notepad.

25 In the list box click Paintbrush to highlight its entry then click the Switch To button.

SECTION 5
Essential skills

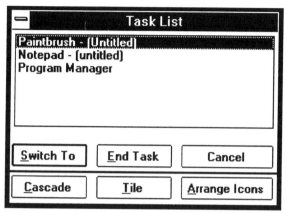

Task List

Keyboard alternative – Use the direction keys to highlight the entry for paintbrush and press Enter.

Task List disappears and the Paintbrush window is brought to the front.

6 Maximise Paintbrush.

Keyboard alternative – Alt-Spacebar, X.

7 Use Ctrl-Esc again to see the Task list.

Keyboard alternative – Ctrl-Esc.

61

■ SECTION 5
Essential skills

28 Select Program Manager in the list and click Switch To.

Keyboard alternative – Highlight Program Manager in the list and press Enter.

29 Maximise the Program Manager window.

Keyboard alternative – Alt-Spacebar, X.

Instead of three icons representing open applications we now have three maximised windows. Obviously only one is visible, the other two are in the background. To switch from one maximised window to another you can use Ctrl-Esc to see the Task List. A quicker method, however, is through the Alt-Tab combination (Alt-Esc is similar in its operation).

30 Press and hold down the Alt key. Press the Tab key a few times with Alt kept down. You will cycle through the three application windows. Try and end up with the Program Manager window current.

Keyboard alternative – Alt(held down)-Tab.

Alt-Tab is normally quicker than Ctrl-Esc unless you have a lot of applications running, in which case the cycling may take some time. There is a nice variation of the Alt-Tab combination which is ideal if most of your work involves repeatedly moving between just two of the applications.

SECTION 5
Essential skills

31 Press and hold down the Alt key. While it is depressed press the Tab key repeatedly until you see the Notepad title bar and then let go of both keys. Repeat this step for Paintbrush.

Keyboard alternative – Alt(held down)-Tab.

32 Press and hold the Alt key and then press the Tab key and let go of both immediately. You will cycle from Paintbrush to Notepad (or vice versa).

Keyboard alternative – Alt-Tab.

33 Repeat step 32 to see Paintbrush again (or Notepad). You can repeat step 32 as many times as you like, but you will notice that Program Manager has been dropped from the sequence. To re-introduce Program Manager to the sequence you will need to use Alt-Tab as in step 30.

Keyboard alternative – Alt-Tab.

Alt-Tab (let go of Tab only) cycles through all open applications. Alt-Tab (let go of both) cycles between the last two applications only. You can alter the default two applications by using Alt-Tab until you find one of the applications you want and then letting go of Tab. Repeat this for the second application you wish to work on. These are the new defaults and you can utilise Alt-Tab (let go of both) to cycle between these two only.

So far we have looked at multiple applications as icons and as full windows. There are yet more alternatives, for example having two or more windows moved and sized in such a manner that you

SECTION 5
Essential skills

have two or more windows completely visible at the same time. This is called tiling. Or you might prefer to have overlapping windows with a portion of each window just showing behind the ones on top. This is referred to as cascading. Tiling and cascading of open application windows can be done through the Task List (by clicking Tile and Cascade respectively in the Task List window). We are going to do it manually, as this will involve practice in moving and sizing windows. To summarise - the modes of working include icons, full windows, tiling and cascading. And of course you can combine any or all of these at the same time. The exact mode you eventually adopt is entirely down to personal preference and the demands of the current session.

Working with multiple applications has great benefits. The more memory in your computer the more applications you can have open, though there is no reason why you should not work with one application at a time if you wish. Perhaps the greatest single benefit of working with multiple applications is that while one application is tied up in printing (or lengthy processing) you can switch to another application and continue working. This is an example of multi-tasking, though there is still some debate about the exact meaning of the term multi-tasking.

If you wish to multi-task many large Windows-based applications, say Excel, Ventura, Word for Windows and Superbase, then a 386 machine with more than two megabytes of RAM is advisable. This does not, though, preclude those readers with 286 and 8086 computers, perhaps with one megabyte or less of RAM, from carrying out a limited degree of multi-tasking. If you wish to multi-task non-Windows applications alongside Windows accessories and Windows-based applications then a 386 or 486 computer is necessary.

SECTION 5
Essential skills

One popular method of working is to tile two applications horizontally, clicking the window of the other application when you want to switch. This is also a useful arrangement when you wish to transfer data from one of the applications to the other. This data transfer between applications is known as clipboarding.

34 Make Paintbrush current with Alt-Tab and click the restore button to reduce it from its full window. You should see Notepad, or possibly Program Manager, behind the Paintbrush window.

Keyboard alternative – Alt-Tab, Alt-Spacebar, R.

35 Repeat step 34 with Notepad.

Keyboard alternative – Alt-Tab, Alt-Spacebar, R.

6 Make Program Manager current with Alt-Tab (or you can just click its window if you can see it), restore it first *and* then minimise it. We are tucking Program Manager away as an icon just to make the display less cluttered.

Keyboard alternative – Alt-Tab, Alt-Spacebar, N.

7 Make Paintbrush current with Alt-Tab (or click the Paintbrush window if you can see it).

SECTION 5
Essential skills

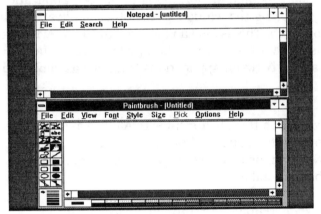
Horizontal tiling

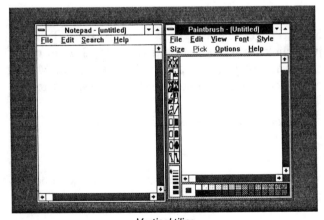
Vertical tiling

■ SECTION 5
Essential skills

Keyboard alternative – Alt-Tab.

38 Place the mouse pointer on the title bar of Paintbrush and drag the mouse. You should detect a corresponding movement of the Paintbrush window on screen. Continue dragging until the Paintbrush title bar is flush with the top of the screen.

Keyboard alternative – Alt-Spacebar, M, Up arrow, Enter. Use the Up arrow key until the title bar is in position and press Enter to anchor this position.

39 Place the mouse pointer on the lower border of Paintbrush. The pointer will change into a double-headed arrow. When you see this double-headed arrow drag the mouse up or down until the border is about half way down the screen.

Keyboard alternative – Alt-Spacebar, S, Down arrow, Up arrow, Enter. Here the Down arrow key is used to select which border to move in order to resize the window. Down arrow selects the border at the bottom. The second direction key, in this example Up, indicates the direction in which you wish to move the selected border. Once again Enter is for anchoring the final position of the border.

40 Place the mouse pointer on the left border and drag the mouse to the left until the left border is flush with the left edge of your display. If the left border is actually off the screen you will first have to drag the whole window to the

■ SECTION 5
Essential skills

right. You do so by dragging on the title bar of the Paintbrush window.

Keyboard alternative – Alt-Spacebar, S, Left arrow, Left arrow, Enter.

41 Adapt step 40 to align the right border of Paintbrush with the right of the screen. Hopefully Paintbrush is nicely positioned in the top half of your display.

Keyboard alternative – Alt-Spacebar, S, Right arrow, Right arrow, Enter.

42 Click Notepad to bring it to the front (or use Alt-Tab if it happens to be hidden behind Paintbrush).

Keyboard alternative – Alt-Tab.

43 Place the mouse pointer on the lower border of Notepad's window and drag the border up so that the height of the Notepad window is slightly less than half the height of your screen.

Keyboard alternative – Alt-Spacebar, S, Down, Up (or Down), Enter.

44 Place the pointer on the title bar of Notepad and drag its window until the top border is immediately below the lower

■ SECTION 5
Essential skills

border of Paintbrush. The lower border of Notepad should be just above the bottom of the screen.

Keyboard alternative – Alt-Spacebar, M, Down, Enter.

15 Drag the left border of Notepad so that it aligns with the left of the screen.

Keyboard alternative – Alt-Spacebar, S, Left, Left, Enter.

16 Drag the right border of Notepad to the right of the screen.

Keyboard alternative – Alt-Spacebar, S, Right, Right, Enter.

Notepad and Paintbrush are now tiled horizontally. If, say, you are waiting for a Paintbrush graphic to print you could click Notepad and type in some text. Practice moving and sizing the two windows until they a little smaller than full screen yet slightly offset so they overlap. The two applications are now cascaded. Switching from front to hidden window is simply a matter of clicking the visible section of the partially hidden window.

17 Switch to Paintbrush by clicking its window or using Alt-Tab.

Keyboard alternative – Alt-Tab.

■ SECTION 5
Essential skills

48 Maximise Paintbrush by clicking its maximise button. Take a break and create a masterpiece in Paintbrush.

Keyboard alternative – Alt-Spacebar, X. You will find Paintbrush is not so easy to use without the mouse. If you can not wait to paint a picture either try Alt-H, K or jump ahead to the section on Paintbrush, which contains some hints on keyboard operations.

Incidentally Paintbrush and Solitaire are excellent for practising standard Windows techniques (at least that is my excuse for playing Solitaire). Reversi is fun but not so useful as it involves no dragging (and I always seem to lose to the computer).

49 Close both Paintbrush and Notepad by double clicking their Control menus. If you are asked if you want to save your work, click no. I am glibly assuming you have not actually created a masterpiece in Paintbrush yet.

Keyboard alternative – Alt-Spacebar, C.

50 Restore the Program Manager icon to a window by double clicking.

Keyboard alternative – Alt-Spacebar, R.

51 In Program Manager close the Accessories window by double clicking its Control menu.

Keyboard alternative – Alt-Hyphen, N.

SECTION 5
Essential skills

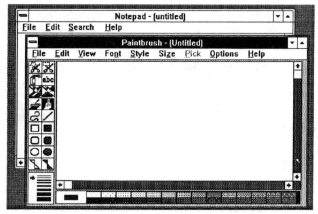
An example of cascading

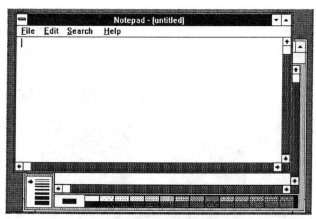
Another example of cascading

SECTION 5
Essential skills

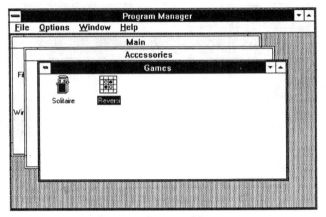

Cascading Program Manager

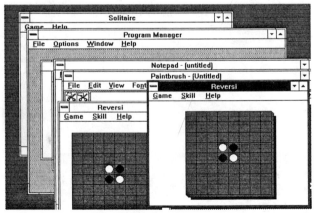

Too much cascading

■ SECTION 5
Essential skills

A note on Program Manager

If you maximise a group or document window it takes over the whole of the Program Manager window. It will not maximise to full screen, as an application window would, unless Program Manager itself is running full screen. However it will overlay other group windows and icons. You can cycle hidden group windows and icons with the Ctrl-Tab key combination. This works in the same way as Alt-Tab does for application windows and icons. You can also restore the maximised group window to its original size by clicking its restore button – the one containing the double arrow heads. It is directly below the maximise/restore button for Program Manager itself and is at the end of the Program Manager menu bar. Ctrl-Tab is the Windows convention for cycling document windows and icons. Alt-Tab is the convention for cycling application windows and icons. An alternative to Ctrl-Tab is to use the Windows option on the Program Manager menu bar.

Menus, list and dialogue boxes

The following set of exercises is designed to make you acquainted with most of the remaining Windows techniques, actions and conventions. In particular you will be looking at pull-down menus, list and dialogue boxes.

1 In Program Manager double click the Accessories group icon to restore it to a window.

Keyboard alternative – Ctrl-Tab to highlight Accessories, then press Enter. Or you could try Alt-W, 5, though you might require a different number from 5.

SECTION 5
Essential skills

2 Double click the application icon for Notepad to open a window for Notepad.

Keyboard alternative – Move to the Notepad icon with the direction keys and press Enter.

3 Maximise Notepad by clicking its maximise button.

Keyboard alternative – Alt-Spacebar, X.

4 Click File in the Notepad menu bar to access the File pull-down menu.

Keyboard alternative – Alt-F.

There are a number of entries in this menu. In particular note the option called Open. This has three dots after it, the term for the dots is *ellipsis*. An ellipsis in a menu choice indicates further information must be provided by the user before the command is implemented, in this case opening a file. The extra information is entered in the subsequent dialogue box.

5 Click the Edit option in the menu bar and take a look at the choices in the Edit pull-down menu.

Keyboard alternative – Alt-E.

You should see that Undo and a few other options are in faint type. Such entries are said to be grayed or dimmed and are not

SECTION 5
Essential skills

available for selection. Some other action must be carried out first before it becomes undimmed. Undo, for example, lets you undo your previous activity in the workspace. However, there has been no activity yet and Undo is therefore not yet available. Next to the option for Time/Date is an entry F5. This is a keyboard shortcut. These shortcuts are especially appropriate when your hands are on the keyboard, perhaps you are typing in text or numeric data. Simply hitting the F5 function key inserts system date and time at the current location of the cursor. Otherwise you would have to reach for the mouse and click Edit followed by Time/Date. If you click the final choice in this menu for Word Wrap the whole menu disappears. Clicking Edit once more shows a tick (check mark) next to Word Wrap. Clicking Word Wrap a second time removes the check mark. This type of menu selection is called a toggle. Toggles are clicked to turn them on and off. Word Wrap, by the way, causes the text to wrap at the right side of the screen instead of continuing off the edge. The final type of menu entry, which you will encounter only rarely, has a black triangle next to it. This is the mark of a cascading menu. A menu option that cascades summons an additional menu to the side.

In quite a few Windows-based applications you will also encounter a slightly different kind of toggle. This is the Short Menus/Full Menus toggle and is worth using. To see complete pull-down menus containing all options that are available select Full Menus. To shorten the menus to leave only the most popular options displayed select Short Menus. If you have Full Menus selected the toggle shows as Short Menus and vice versa.

6 Click File then click Open in the File pull-down menu. As Open is followed by an ellipsis, clicking Open leads to a dialogue box where you can provide additional information.

SECTION 5
Essential skills

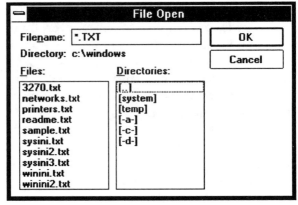

File Open dialogue

Keyboard alternative – Alt-F, O.

The File Open dialogue box partially overlays the Notepad window. It has its own Control menu. This contains two options, for closing or moving the dialogue. With the mouse it is easier to close a dialogue box by clicking Cancel. Cancel leaves the previous default settings intact. To move the dialogue box with the mouse you drag it by its title bar. Clicking OK in a dialogue box also closes the dialogue but registers any changes you may have made to the contents. Most dialogue boxes observe the same conventions. This dialogue box also includes a number of standard Windows features. There are a couple of additional features not shown in this File Open dialogue, but these will be covered shortly.

The dialogue does contain a text box, labelled Filename. Text boxes allow you to type in text, here you might want to type in the name of a file you wish to open. There are two list boxes. List

SECTION 5
Essential skills

boxes, as the name suggests, contain lists, from which you can choose the list entry you require. The two list boxes are labelled Files and Directories. OK and Cancel are examples of command buttons. In addition there is an information line, labelled Directory. This tells you the name of the current directory. Your dialogue box might have another feature, this will depend upon the number of directories on the current drive and the number of files in the current directory. This additional feature would be a scroll bar, or perhaps two of them. Do not worry if your dialogue box is without scroll bars. To move from one feature to another in a dialogue box involves clicking the feature with the mouse. Keyboard users have the alternative of pressing Tab, or Shift-Tab, to cycle round the features – Shift-Tab cycles in reverse. A more direct keyboard method is to press and hold down Alt while pressing the letter of the desired label, though some command pushbuttons do not have an underlined letter.

The text box should be highlighted and will have the entry *.TXT. This tells Notepad to display all files with a TXT extension, found in the current directory, in the Files list box below. If you want to see all the files with a BAT extension you type *.BAT. *.BAT will only directly replace *.TXT if *.TXT is highlighted. You can highlight text in a text box, if the highlight is not already there, by dragging the mouse across the text. Or you can position the cursor in the text box by clicking it and changing the current entry with Backspace and Delete keys, then typing the replacement. If you experiment make sure the entry is put back to *.TXT. With the keyboard you cycle to a text box with Tab or Shift-Tab or jump directly with Alt-letter.

List box to the left is the one containing all the files in the current directory that match the filename, or filename template, in the Filename text box. Something like MYFILE.TXT is a filename and *.TXT is a template. The current directory is shown on the

■ SECTION 5
Essential skills

information line. You use a list box to choose alternatives; here it is used to stipulate a file to open. Choosing with a mouse involves clicking the filename then clicking OK, or you can simply double click the filename. Choosing with the keyboard, after cycling or jumping to the list box, is done by moving the highlight to the choice with the direction keys (Up and Down arrows) then pressing Enter. In some situations you are required to make a multiple choice in a list box. With the mouse this is accomplished by single clicking each of the choices in turn and clicking OK when all the choices have been made. To remove one of the choices from the list click it. With the keyboard move to each choice in turn and press the Spacebar. Pressing Spacebar a second time on one of the choices will cancel its selection. Quite often lists are too long to fit in the space for the list box. Then you see vertical scroll bars at the side of the list box. With the keyboard you use direction keys to scroll hidden entries into view. With the mouse you click the up or down arrows at the top and bottom of the scroll bar. If *.TXT is still in the text box you see all files with a TXT extension in the current directory. Should you not be in the default Windows directory you might have no files at all in the list box. It is important that you know how to change the current directory, especially when searching for files to open. The list box on the right is designed to allow you to do just that.

This second list box follows exactly the same conventions as the list box on the left. You may or may not have a scroll bar to the side, this depends upon the number of drives and directories you have. To change drive you choose the letter for the drive. If you can not see letters for [a] and [c] – there may also be further letters – scroll down the list. Remember that choosing from a list box is click then OK, or double click, or highlight then press Enter. Once you are logged onto the correct drive you can move around directories on that drive. Directories actually listed are sub-directories of the current directory on the current drive. You move

SECTION 5
Essential skills

into a subdirectory by choosing it. Often you may want to switch to a directory at the same level as the current directory. In order to do this it is necessary to back through the directory tree to the next highest level and come down the required branch. Backing through a directory tree is done by choosing the double dot [..]. If you choose this one repeatedly you end up in the root directory of the current drive. We eventually want to finish up in your default Windows directory, you are probably there already, and this will be indicated on the information line. Yours may well be C:\WINDOWS, but not necessarily - the exact drive and directory name are those specified during installation. If you are not sure of the correct directory, the default Windows directory contains a number of files with the TXT extension (README.TXT, NETWORKS.TXT, PRINTERS.TXT and so on). These should be listed in the list box on the left.

Command buttons in this dialogue are for OK and Cancel. Cancel always backs you out of a dialogue and leaves original settings intact, useful if you call one up accidentally. OK accepts settings in the dialogue. Choosing a command button with the mouse is done by clicking. From the keyboard you can cycle to the relevant button with Tab and press Enter. If the command contains an underlined letter, it is possible to jump straight to the command by pressing Alt-letter. A command button with a heavier outline than others is currently selected and can be activated simply by pressing Enter. A button with an ellipsis, opens another separate dialogue box. A button with a double chevron (>>) expands the current dialogue. A keyboard shortcut for choosing a Cancel button is to press Esc.

■ SECTION 5
Essential skills

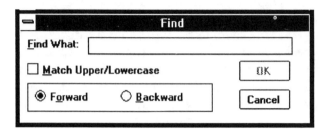

Find dialogue

7 Open the file called README.TXT in the default Windows directory by double clicking its name.

Keyboard alternative – Alt-F to jump to the list box, then Down arrow to select README.TXT and finally press Enter.

8 Click Search on the Notepad menu bar then click Find. This displays the Find dialogue.

Keyboard alternative – Alt-S, F.

9 Type **to** in the text box.

Keyboard alternative – Type **to**.

Underneath this you see a check box labelled Match Upper/Lowercase. The check box should be empty, that is it is not selected. When selected a check box displays a cross in the box. This particular check box helps to narrow the criteria of the

SECTION 5
Essential skills

search. When selected it performs a case-sensitive search for the entry in the text box. To select a check box with the mouse you click the box. Repeat this to turn off the check box. With the keyboard first cycle or jump to the check box then press Spacebar to turn the box on or off.

0 Turn on the checkbox for Match Upper/Lowercase.

Keyboard alternative – Alt-M.

Below the checkbox are two circular buttons called option buttons. In some applications manuals they are referred to as radio buttons. They differ from check boxes in that they are mutually exclusive, you can not choose two option buttons in the same group. Multiple check boxes in a group are not subject to this restriction, you can turn on as many as you wish. The option buttons in question instruct Notepad to search either forwards or backwards through the text, from the current cursor location: it can not search forwards and backwards at the same time. We want to search forwards in this example, the cursor being at the start of the document. Default setting is forwards though it is worth having a go with the option buttons. Once again you simply click with the mouse to turn option buttons on and off. From the keyboard you cycle to the option button group and use the direction keys to turn on and off. A keyboard shortcut is Alt-letter.

1 Turn on the backward button.

Keyboard alternative – Alt-B.

■ SECTION 5
Essential skills

12   Turn on the forward button.

Keyboard alternative – Alt-O.

13   Choose OK.

Keyboard alternative – Enter.

The word *to* in the first sentence is now highlighted. Note the word *TO* in the title has been skipped over, a result of the Match Upper/Lowercase check box being operative.

Notice the scroll bars at the foot and to the right of the Notepad window. They are there to help you move around the text (or graphic, database or spreadsheet, depending on the application). With the mouse you could click the desired cursor position, but this desired location may not be visible. At the end of each scroll bar is a scroll arrow. Clicking an arrow moves you by increments in the direction of the arrow. In each scroll bar there is a scroll box. Clicking the scroll bar outside the scroll box moves you vertically or horizontally, though by a much greater distance than the scroll arrows. Dragging a scroll box along a scroll bar allows you to reach a desired position quickly. For example dragging the box all the way down the vertical scroll bar takes you to the end of the document, dragging the box in the horizontal bar sweeps left and right.

SECTION 5
Essential skills

Working with text

All Windows accessories and applications observe similar conventions when it comes to working with text.

There are conventions for moving around in text documents and for selecting text. Once text is selected it is manipulated in various ways. For example, it can be retrospectively formatted, or moved or copied. Text conventions apply to text entries in spreadsheets and databases, not only to text editors and word processors.

To move cursor position with the mouse you click the desired location. If the new location is not in the current screen, then use the scroll bars to scroll to the correct point. Some applications have a Goto option (through the menu bar) which enables you to jump to a specified page number.

Moving within text via the keyboard depends upon where you want to move to. The usual conventions are set up in the table on the following page. If your hands are on the keyboard anyway, you might be typing, then even if you have a mouse the keyboard options are often more convenient.

When entering text the Spacebar forces a gap of one character width, Enter forces the cursor to begin a new line. Mistakes are rectified with the Delete and Backspace keys. Former deletes the character right of the cursor, latter the character to the left. Once text has been selected Delete removes all selected text. Many applications have an undo option on the edit menu which retrieves accidentally deleted text, as long as you do nothing else in between. The keyboard shortcut for undo is Alt-Backspace. To insert text in existing text, position the cursor and type. The existing text moves to the right and down to accommodate the new text. Most applications (though not Notepad) have an over-

SECTION 5
Essential skills

type facility. Overtype means new text actually overwrites existing text as you type. Overtype is turned on by pressing Insert. This key is a toggle and pressing it again turns off overtype, and restores the default insert mode.

New location	Keyboard method
Next character	Right arrow
Previous character	Left arrow
Next word	Ctrl-Right arrow
Previous word	Ctrl-Left arrow
Next line	Down arrow
Previous line	Up arrow
Next window of text (down)	Page Down
Previous window of text (up)	Page Up
Next window of text (right)	Ctrl-Page Down
Previous window of text (left)	Ctrl-Page Up
End of line	End
Start of line	Home
End of all text	Ctrl-End
Start of all text	Ctrl-Home

Moving within text

To select text with the mouse drag the mouse over the text. In many applications you can select a word by double clicking the word. One alternative to dragging is to click at the start or finish of selected text then to press the Shift key as you click at the opposite end. Windows word processors normally give you an extensive range of options for selecting text. Notepad is not really

SECTION 5
Essential skills

a word processor, it is more of a text editor, and its facilities for selecting text are limited. Write, a basic word processor bundled with Windows, has more options. To select a line in Write, for instance, you click to the left of it.

To select an area of text with the keyboard, position the cursor at the start or finish of the block of text. Then while holding down the Shift key use the direction keys to move to the other. The Shift key may be used with keyboard methods of moving through text, given in the table, to easily extend selection.

As already mentioned, selected text may be then be formatted, moved or copied. Text can be moved or copied within the current document or to another document, and even into another application. To copy text try Edit then Copy, which copies the text to the Clipboard. Place the cursor at the destination point, this can be in a completely different application if you wish, and choose Edit followed by Paste. Moving text is an almost identical procedure, except you choose Cut rather than Copy.

Using Help

Accessories that accompany Windows, and the vast majority of Windows applications, have an extremely useful help feature. This is always accessed by clicking Help or pressing Alt-H (a keyboard shortcut is F1). From the pull-down menu, Index provides a gateway to an onboard manual. And depending upon application you might well see other Help options. Some applications come with an onboard tutorial, for instance. Again depending upon the application, the Shift-F1 key combination may give context sensitive help. This does not apply to the Windows accessories, only to separately purchased applications. Many Help pull-down menus have the Keyboard option which gives information specifically for users without a mouse.

SECTION 5
Essential skills

While you are learning an accessory or other application, the Help window can be sized, moved and left running. That way you have immediate access to help, without impinging too much upon the workspace.

Once you are in Help there a couple of methods of moving through the documentation without returning to the Index all the time. Back, for example retraces your steps and Browse shows topics related to the current topic in the Help window.

1 If Notepad is still on your screen practice moving around the README.TXT document. Try clicking Help, looking up information, then closing Help down. You might find the README.TXT document itself contains some useful information. Practice selecting text. You might like to try Edit, Copy, Paste and Edit, Cut, Paste. Do not worry about messing up the text for we will not keep the alterations you make.

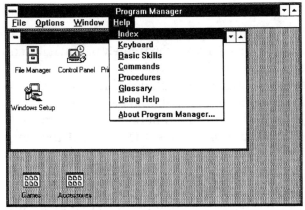

Program Manager Help menu

SECTION 5
Essential skills

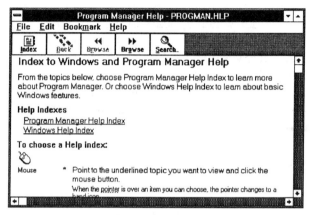

A typical Help window

Keyboard alternative – See the table earlier for keyboard methods of moving through text. Open Help with Alt-H. Close Help with Alt-Spacebar, C. Edit, Copy is Alt-E, C (or Ctrl-Insert). Edit, Cut is Alt-E, T (or Shift-Delete). Edit, Paste is Alt-E, P (or Shift-Insert).

2 Close Notepad by double clicking the Control menu. If you have made any changes at all Notepad asks if you wish to save your changes. Choose No to retain the original document and to lose your changes.

Keyboard alternative – Alt-Spacebar, C. To retain the original document and lose your changes press N in the ensuing dialogue. If you have made no alterations then Notepad closes without putting up a dialogue.

We will be working largely from the accessories group for a while so you may leave that group window open. If you quit Windows

SECTION 5
Essential skills

and wish it to restart with this new arrangement, turn on the Save Changes check box which appears in the Exit Windows dialogue. There is however one more standard Windows attribute to consider and this involves opening Control Panel, which is in the Main group window. You are not obliged to keep these groups and their contents as they stand. Later, in the section: Program Manager, you will see how to customise Windows to meet your own requirements.

Drop-down list boxes

1 Open the Main group window. There is no need to close the accessories window first.

Keyboard alternative – Alt-W, 3 (or the relevant number). If you prefer use the Ctrl-Tab combination to highlight the Main icon and press Enter.

2 Start Control Panel by double clicking its icon. In the Control Panel window is an icon labelled Color.

Keyboard alternative – Highlight the Control Panel icon by pressing the direction keys and press Enter.

3 Double click the Color icon and the Color dialogue box appears.

Keyboard alternative – Highlight the Color icon, if necessary, by pressing the direction keys and press Enter.

SECTION 5
Essential skills

This dialogue is where you alter the colours of your windows. Obviously you need to have a colour monitor to appreciate the results. That is not the point of this exercise, however, which is to demonstrate use of drop-down list boxes. All the list boxes we have met so far hold a maximum of six to ten entries. If there are more entries than the maximum available then Windows adds a scroll bar to the side, allowing you to scroll the hidden entries into view. In some dialogues, though, full list boxes are inappropriate, usually because of space limitations. Instead Windows has drop-down list boxes. These initially display only one list item and to the right of this is an underlined down arrow.

> To open the full list box click this underlined down arrow with the mouse. From the keyboard press Alt-Down arrow. To see alternatives in the list one by one, press Down arrow or Up arrow. You can then make a choice from the list as normal. To hide a drop-down list, click the arrow again or press Alt-Down arrow a second time. There may still be too many entries in a drop-down list, in which case use the scroll bar as usual to move through the list.

Drop-down list

SECTION 5
Essential skills

4 Open the drop-down list box for Color Schemes and scroll through the list.

Keyboard alternative – Alt-Down arrow (Alt-Up also works), and then Down and Up arrow keys to scroll.

5 Close the drop-down list.

Keyboard alternative – Alt-Down (or Alt-Up).

6 Click Cancel to leave the dialogue. Or click OK if you have a colour monitor and wish to alter the Windows colour scheme. Fluorescent is worth trying, for a couple of minutes. The standard colour scheme is called Windows Default, as I am sure you will not want to keep fluorescent, though some of the others are rather more restful!

Keyboard alternative – Press Esc.

7 Close Control Panel by double clicking its Control menu.

Keyboard alternative – Alt-Spacebar, C.

8 Minimise the Main group window to an icon, and restore the accessories group, if necessary, to an open window. We will be looking at many of the accessories shortly.

■ SECTION 5
Essential skills

Keyboard alternative – Alt-Hyphen, N to minimise the Main group.

To avoid undue repetition of basic instructions in the rest of the book, it is assumed that you have learnt most of the essential skills. Should you encounter an action you are unable to carry out, refer back to this section on essential skills. Keyboard alternatives, in particular, are normally only mentioned if they have not already been covered in this section.

PART TWO

Accessories

■ SECTION 6
Using the accessories

Windows is not only a GUI, or a pretty operating environment in which to run your major applications. It also comes with its own bundled applications and set of utilities, not to mention a couple of games. Most of the utilities reside in the Main group and the applications in the Accessories group. Though if your copy of Windows has already been customised to an extent, this may no longer be true, they could be anywhere! The two games, Solitaire and Reversi, are in the Games group. If there are any Windows-based applications, for example Excel, that Setup detected during installation then these will be in the Windows Applications group. Standard applications, if any, can be found in the Non-Windows Applications group.

Accessories themselves provide a range of applications suitable for many people. Their use is also an excellent introduction to learning Windows techniques and conventions. Should you ever outgrow the accessories, (they may simply not be powerful or flexible enough to meet your needs), they can be replaced by separately bought Windows-based applications. Part Five contains a discussion of some of the most popular alternatives. Due to limitations on space we can not hope to cover all the accessories in any great depth. If one of the accessories seems interesting to you then access Help freely and consult your Windows User's Guide for further information.

Write is probably one of the most useful of the accessories. This is a basic word processor which is perfectly adequate for most purposes. Should your requirements extend to spell checking and mail merge, then you might later wish to buy a more powerful word processor. Examples include Ami Professional and Word for Windows.

Paintbrush is a graphics program and is great fun to play with. You might use it to design logos or prepare artwork for your

■ SECTION 6
Using the accessories

publications. Later, as your needs become more sophisticated, there are versatile alternatives. Both Corel Draw and Micrografx Designer are worth considering.

Terminal is a communications module. As such it has additional hardware requirements, though once these requirements have been met it is ideal for sending and receiving files, or accessing services like CompuServe. To make a remote connection you need a modem connected to a spare serial port. It is possible that you might want a greater range of terminal emulations and protocols than are available with Terminal. If that is so there are packages like CrossTalk and Dynacomm.

Calculator is, as you might have guessed, a calculator. It provides features normally found on scientific pocket calculators and copes with statistical functions and differing number systems. Although hardly a valid comparison, more complex numeric or financial functions would suggest buying a spreadsheet. The choice here may be Excel or Wingz.

Calendar is a means of keeping and arranging appointments, with a built-in alarm function. If you find Calendar too basic for your needs then applications like Planisoft and IBM Current are available.

Cardfile is a simple flat-file database. You might find it perfect for storing names and addresses of business contacts. Although to avail yourself of powerful relational database features you should invest in something like Superbase 2, Superbase 4 or Omnis 5.

Clock is simply a clock, which may be set to display as an analogue or digital clock. When minimised to an icon it still shows the time; you might wish to tuck it away at the foot of the screen, where it continues to tick away.

■ SECTION 6
Using the accessories

Notepad is a text editor and lacks the features of Write. Having said that it is a handy accessory. It is very convenient for editing plain text files: AUTOEXEC.BAT, CONFIG.SYS, WIN.INI and DOS batch files. These are tricky to edit in a word processor, where you must be careful to preserve their ASCII formats.

Recorder is for recording and playing back macros. If you regularly carry out the same sequence of keystrokes and mouse clicks as you work, then a macro allows you to automate the whole sequence.

PIF Editor is there for fine tuning the manner in which standard applications work in the Windows environment. PIF is an acronym for program information file and such files tell Windows how to treat the application. Windows accessories and utilities do not require a PIF file, nor do Windows-based applications. Most standard applications also run satisfactorily without a PIF. PIFs are generally only required if you wish to multi-task standard applications in Windows enhanced mode, and you wish to maintain tight control over how the applications behave and use memory. Most people can afford to ignore PIFs altogether.

The next section of the book give you a brief introduction to some of the accessories. As this is, as far as possible, a practical book and not a reference manual, it is difficult to cover all options available in all accessories. Once you have gained an introduction to each accessory you are recommended to experiment, to click Help, and to consult the Windows User's Guide.

■ SECTION 7
Applying the accessories

TypeCast plc is a busy desktop publishing agency. In order to produce brochures and other materials TypeCast has copies of PageMaker and Ventura Publisher. Both of these applications run under Windows 3, so TypeCast bought a copy of that too. PageMaker is ideal for brochures, posters and advertising material. Ventura tends to be the choice for the magazines and books TypeCast publishes on behalf of clients. But having bought Windows 3 the employees found a place for the Windows accessories in their day-to-day work.

Being a typical Windows 3 user the company has only Windows-based applications. As such it finds it never looks at PIF Editor. And once the employees opened and closed Clock a couple of times they forgot all about it. But they do make use of the other accessories. Here are some examples of how they do so. Graphics, logos and special artistic effects are created in Paintbrush. These logos are placed into PageMaker and Ventura as part of publications. They are also copied into Write for inclusion in letters to clients, perhaps showing some sample designs. Text for publication is typed up in Write before transfer to the desktop publishing software. Calculations of clients' costs are done in Calculator and pasted into letters to clients prepared in Write. Notes and inter-office memos are quickly knocked up in Notepad, and some of these too find their way into Write letters. Details of clients are kept in Cardfile, and once again the information is sometimes transferred into letters. Calendar is used by TypeCast personnel to record their forthcoming appointments and things-to-do. It also serves for some basic project management. TypeCast is investigating the feasibility of purchasing a modem, at present they do not use Terminal. Finally Recorder is there to automate some of the repetitive work.

TypeCast has recently received a commission from another company, Rectangle and Circle plc, to design a company logo and print

SECTION 7
Applying the accessories

an inhouse newsletter. Rectangle and Circle is a new client and have requested a breakdown of the costs and tasks involved, and to see a preview of the logo design.

To design the logo:

1 Open and maximise Paintbrush. The Paintbrush workspace is divided into four distinct sections. Down the left hand side are the Toolbox icons and beneath them is the Linesize area. Along the bottom is the Palette, the rest of the workspace being taken up by the drawing area. Keyboard users can move around these four areas with the Tab key.

It is worth mentioning some keyboard alternatives here. The Insert key replaces clicking when choosing options in the Toolbox, Linesize area and Palette. F9 with Insert is the equivalent of double clicking and the Delete key is the alternative to right

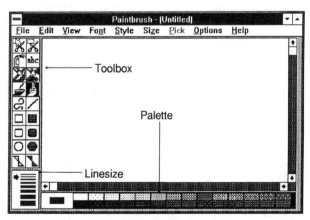

Paintbrush

■ SECTION 7
Applying the accessories

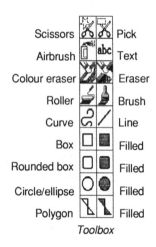
Toolbox

clicking. Right clicking is used in Paintbrush to select a background colour from the Palette. You can move around one of the sections with the direction keys. To choose the Filled Box (Rectangle) tool, for example, Tab to the Toolbox, move the pointer to the tool and press Insert. The equivalent to dragging the mouse is holding down the Insert key and moving with the direction keys. Note that Shift-Page Up is used instead of the normal Ctrl-Page Up to move one window to the right.

If Toolbox and Linesize ever disappear from the display, click View then Tools & Linesize. Clicking View then Palette recalls a missing Palette. If your drawing area ever changes into a series of small squares click View followed by Zoom Out. Small squares indicate that you have inadvertently zoomed in. Zooming in (View, Zoom In) is very convenient for detailed editing work on your graphics.

At the left of the Palette is a small rectangle contained within a larger rectangle. The inner rectangle is the current foreground colour and the outer rectangle is the background colour. The

■ SECTION 7
Applying the accessories

default settings are solid black on white. We will work with the default settings, though to change the foreground colour later click (or press Insert) the desired colour in the Palette. Background colour is changed by right clicking (or by pressing Delete).

2 Click the Filled Box (Rectangle) tool.

3 Position the cursor at the left of the drawing area (use the direction keys if you have no mouse) and drag the mouse to form an area about one inch high by two inches across. Release the mouse button and Paintbrush creates a solid black rectangle. To drag from the keyboard hold down the Insert key while using the direction keys.

4 Click the Filled Circle tool in the Toolbox. Position the cursor at the top right hand corner of the rectangle you have just drawn.

5 Drag the mouse down and to the right, until the cursor forms a square with its first position at the top right of the rectangle. Let go of the button and you should have a circle to the right of the rectangle.

It is not at all important to the exercises if your logo does not look exactly like the logo shown here, all that matters is that you have drawn something. If you feel like starting again click File then New, and when asked if you wish to save the current image choose

■ SECTION 7
Applying the accessories

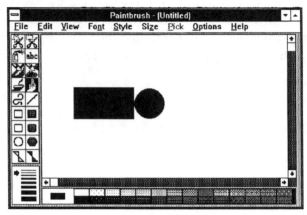

Completed logo

No. A quick way of beginning again is to double click the Eraser tool (or press F9 with Insert with the pointer on the Eraser tool).

As the logo is used later it is vital that it is saved. To save the logo:

1 Click File then Save (Save As is for creating a copy of a file with a different name). File, Save is the method of saving data in all Windows accessories and applications.

The text *.BMP in the text box is highlighted. Typing in a filename will automatically overwrite the selected text. Before you do so check that the directory shown is the one where you wish to store your data. If necessary change the directory in the Directories list box, you might have a specific directory where you hold data files. Changing directory like this removes the highlight from *.BMP. You can re-highlight by dragging and overtype with the filename,

SECTION 7
Applying the accessories

or you will have to edit the text box contents manually with Backspace or Delete.

2 Type **LOGO** as the filename and click OK.

A successful save results in the filename appearing in the title bar of Paintbrush: LOGO.BMP. BMP is the default file extension for Paintbrush files, there is no need to type in the extension yourself. Some Windows applications do not support the BMP format, in which case you might try the PCX format, accessed through the Options button in the File Save As dialogue.

You might like a trial printout of the logo. This is achieved by clicking File then Print and accepting the defaults in the subsequent dialogue by clicking OK. For a full explanation of the settings in the dialogue refer to the Windows User's Guide. Nearly all Windows accessories and applications have the File, Print routine.

3 Close Paintbrush by double clicking the Control menu. If you have made any alterations to the graphic since saving it, Paintbrush asks if you wish to save the changes. Respond with Yes if you want to keep the changes, No if you do not.

The next set of exercises involves writing a TypeCast internal memo in Notepad. The contents of the memo are copied into Write as part of the letter to Rectangle and Circle.

■ SECTION 7
Applying the accessories

1 Open and maximise Notepad.

2 Click Edit then Word Wrap.

3 Type the following:

> **To: John**
>
> **From: Louise**
>
> **John, when you write to Rectangle and Circle, could you add something to the effect:**
>
> **As part of our fifth anniversary celebrations we are**

The memo in Notepad

SECTION 7
Applying the accessories

> pleased to announce a five percent discount to selected clients only. Please deduct five percent accordingly from any prices quoted.

In a real office situation this memo would probably be printed out and sent to the recipient. If the computers in the office are connected the memo could go directly from Louise's to John's computer, using the Terminal accessory.

4 Click File then Save.

5 Enter the name **MEMO** in the text box and click OK. The file is now called MEMO.TXT, Notepad adds the extension for you.

6 Close Notepad.

Because Rectangle and Circle asked for a breakdown of the work involved it is appropriate to look at Calendar, and to prepare a timetable.

1 Open Calendar.

■ SECTION 7
Applying the accessories

2 Click the right arrow button next to the date to move a few days ahead. The keyboard alternative is Ctrl-Page Down.

3 Click or tab to the scratch pad area at the bottom.

4 Type **Provisional schedule for the Rectangle and Circle inhouse newsletter.**

5 Click in or tab to the main section. You can move from one time to another with the Up and Down arrow keys if you do not possess a mouse.

6 Position the cursor next to 9:00 and type **Type your text in Word for Windows.** Copy the entries in the table.

Time	Text entry
10:00	Put your sales figures into Superbase
11:00	Export figures to Excel and chart
12:00	Place logo and text into PageMaker
13:00	Lunch break
14:00	Place Excel chart in PageMaker
15:00	Place Superbase report in PageMaker
16:00	Laser print newsletter
17:00	Bind newsletter

SECTION 7
Applying the accessories

Calendar

7 Click File, Save and name the calendar file **RECT**. It is automatically assigned a CAL extension as you click OK.

8 Close Calendar.

As TypeCast work on the Rectangle and Circle project they might refer to this timetable. Its contents will be eventually be typed up in a letter, so it can also be used as a reference.

Another task which is quite likely to occur in such a business situation is recording details of Rectangle and Circle in a client database. Cardfile is the obvious choice for this task.

1 Open Cardfile.

■ SECTION 7
Applying the accessories

2 Click Card then Add to see the Add dialogue.

3 Type **RECTANGLE AND CIRCLE** in the text box and click OK.

You are now presented with an index card bearing the title RECTANGLE AND CIRCLE, with the cursor positioned on the first line of the card.

4 Type

> **Rectangle and Circle**
> **Foundry Square**
> **London**

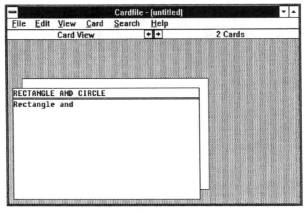

Cardfile

SECTION 7
Applying the accessories

5 Click File then Save and call the file **CLIENTS**. This will be given a CRD extension. Click OK.

In normal usage there might well be dozens of index cards (each added with Card, Add) which are shown in an overlapping stack. You move through the cards by clicking titles of cards. The clicked card comes to the front where it is possible to see all details on the card. View, List shows the data in a list rather than in a stack of cards. Search, Go To is for jumping straight to a card that may not be visible in the window, simply type in the title. Search, Find will locate a card with specified text on the main body of the card. The latter is useful if you remember the name of an individual but not the company under which they are filed.

6 Close Cardfile.

Before we actually write the letter to Rectangle and Circle we are going to record a macro. The macro is to automatically insert a sign off at the end of the letter when it is prepared. It is of course easier to type the sign off directly in the letter. But if you are going to repeat a task many times, for example adding your sign off to many letters, then ultimately a macro saves time and expedites repetitive tasks more easily. Macros can be a little tricky at first. If your attempt should fail then repeat the steps involved, otherwise you can always add the sign off manually later. Before you begin the macro close every accessory and application, apart from Program Manager of course. It is not absolutely necessary to close applications before recording a macro, it just makes the risk of failure less likely until you become more proficient in the use of macros.

■ SECTION 7
Applying the accessories

1 Close everything apart from Program Manager. Open the Accessories group window, if not already open. Read steps 2 to 19 before you try them.

2 Open and maximise Recorder.

3 Click Macro followed by Record.

4 In the ensuing dialogue box access the drop-down list for Shortcut Key and scroll through the list until you see F10.

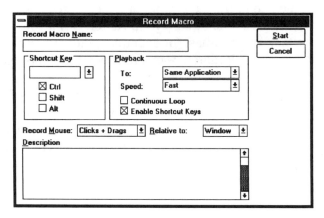

Recorder

■ SECTION 7
Applying the accessories

5 Choose F10 and make sure that the check box for Ctrl is on. At the same time make sure that the check boxes for Shift and Alt are off. This means that the macro can be played back by pressing Ctrl-F10. If the macro does not work and you start the procedure again it is probably easier to choose another key combination, say Ctrl-F9, rather than delete the initial choice.

6 Click the Start button in the dialogue and the Recorder window is minimised to leave only Program Manager running in a window.

7 Press Alt-F then R. Keyboard alternatives are preferable to mouse actions when recording macros. Alt-F, R pulls down the File menu in Program Manager and chooses Run.

8 In the Run dialogue type **Notepad** and press Enter. This action opens the Notepad accessory, provided your Windows directory is either current or on the DOS Path. Both should in fact be true.

9 In the Notepad window type

Yours sincerely,

■ SECTION 7
Applying the accessories

John Font.

Use the Enter key to insert blank lines between the two typed lines.

10 Press Ctrl-Home to take the cursor back to the start.

11 While pressing and holding down Shift press the Ctrl-End combination to highlight all the text. Ctrl-End takes you to the end of a document. Shift is used to make a selection between the two cursor positions.

12 Press Alt-E then C. These actions choose Copy on the Edit menu. The contents of Notepad have now been copied to the Windows Clipboard.

13 Press Alt-Spacebar then C. This closes Notepad.

14 Press N for No when asked if you wish to save your changes.

15 Press Ctrl-Break. This is the key combination that temporarily stops the recording of the macro and through a

SECTION 7
Applying the accessories

dialogue asks if you want to resume recording or stop completely.

16 Click the Save Macro option button, we do not want to resume, then click OK.

17 Double click the Recorder icon to restore the Recorder window. In the window you will see Ctrl-F10, the keyboard shortcut for this particular macro.

18 Click File then Save and call the macro file **SIGNOFF**. Windows will add the REC extension. Click OK to confirm the save.

19 Double click the Recorder Control menu to close it down.

John Font of TypeCast need never type in his sign off again, all he has to do is open Recorder and press Ctrl-F10 and his sign off is ready on the Clipboard for pasting into a word processor. This particular macro is, in reality, probably more trouble than it is worth. Macros, however, when carefully planned and sensibly applied are very helpful. It would pay you to practice creating some macros of your own. There is a lot of advice and information in the Windows User's Guide. Macros, among many other things, are especially suited to recording a series of actions and replaying those actions as part of a software training session.

■ SECTION 7
Applying the accessories

Let us now begin to put everything together in a letter from TypeCast to Rectangle and Circle.

1 Make the Accessories group window current. You can use Ctrl-Tab if it is hidden or minimise a group window like Main to uncover it.

2 Open and maximise Write. The cursor will be ready at the top of the new document.

3 Type the following text:

> **TypeCast plc**
>
> **Fleet Street**
>
> **London**
>
>
> **Dear Jane,**
>
> **Thanks for your call earlier today. I hope this will answer most of your queries.**
>
> **Yes, your company logo is finished and here it is!**

SECTION 7
Applying the accessories

I think you will agree it was well worth waiting for. The intention is for it to give a subtle reference to the name Rectangle and Circle. I hope you can see it.

Once we receive your text and figures by the early morning fax we can have the newsletter back to you by six. This is our publishing schedule:

```
 9:00  Type your text in Word for Windows
10:00  Put your sales figures into Superbase
11:00  Export figures to Excel and chart
12:00  Place logo and text into PageMaker
13:00  Lunch Break
14:00  Place Excel chart in PageMaker
15:00  Place Superbase report in PageMaker
16:00  Laser print newsletter
17:00  Bind newsletter
```

The costs are as follows:

Publication   £1000

Design of logo £8000

TOTAL   £

PS

The exact point for line breaks is unimportant, yours may be different. Though try using the Tab key to line-up the entries in the schedule. Unfortunately you can not copy all of the schedule

SECTION 7
Applying the accessories

from Calendar into Write. The text has to be re-typed, though you could always open the Calendar file and use it as a reference. One way of doing this is to tile both Write and Calendar on screen. The schedule is saved as RECT.CAL and you access it by clicking File then Open in Calendar. You have to be in the correct directory to see RECT.CAL in the list box. Double clicking RECT.CAL opens that file. Calendar opens on today's date and you have to move forward (or backward) to find the day of the schedule.

So far Write, a word processor, seems little more exciting than Notepad, a text editor. Therefore we will experiment with just a few of the features of Write.

4 Drag the mouse over *TypeCast plc, Fleet Street, London* in order to select it. Just as a reminder, keyboard users should press Shift while pressing the direction keys to select text.

5 Click Paragraph then Centered.

6 With the same text still highlighted click Character followed by Bold.

7 And still with the same text selected click Character followed by Fonts. The Font dialogue appears with a Fonts list box to the left and a Sizes list box to the right.

SECTION 7
Applying the accessories

8 Choose Helv or another font in the Fonts list.

9 Choose a point size of 14, or a similar size, from the Size list. You might have to scroll the list first. Click OK.

10 Select the word *TOTAL* in the letter.

11 Click Character then Bold.

12 Click File and then Save. Type **JANE** in the text box for the filename. Make sure none of the check boxes are on before clicking OK to save the letter. Windows automatically appends the WRI extension.

There is obviously a lot more to Write than we have space to consider. Once again you are referred to the relevant chapter in the Windows User's Manual, and a later section on Write in this book.

The letter is not quite complete. It needs the logo pasting in, the name and address of Rectangle and Circle, the sign off, a message about discounts, and a figure to represent the total cost of the job. The logo, name and address, sign off, and message have already been created and are saved in Paintbrush, Cardfile, Recorder and Notepad respectively. Those four applications have been closed down. In a normal working session there is no reason

■ SECTION 7
Applying the accessories

why you should not keep two or even more applications running simultaneously. This obviates the need to keep opening and closing. There is however a limit, and as you begin to run short on memory Windows slows down and occasionally fails to respond to certain instructions. If this should ever happen then you have to shut one or more of the currently open applications. The figure for the total costs is to be worked out in Calculator and pasted into the letter. As you go through the next set of exercises I leave it up to you whether you close applications or not. Though for the sign off, which is a macro, I suggest that you have only Program Manager open right now.

To replay the macro and get the sign off ready on the Clipboard:

1 Make the Accessories group window current and start Recorder.

2 Click File then Open.

3 Choose SIGNOFF.REC from the list box. Remember you may double click or click then select OK.

4 Minimise Recorder so you have a clearer view of what is hopefully about to happen.

■ SECTION 7
Applying the accessories

5 Press Ctrl-F10 to replay the macro. If you had two or more shots at the macro your key combination might well be different. Sit back and relax as the macro takes the pain out of Windows! When you notice the Notepad window disappearing from the screen you know the macro has finished.

This is not a good place to take a break. The sign off is stored on the Clipboard. Clipboard is purely a temporary rest for data. Its contents are lost if you exit Windows or put something new on the Clipboard. It is possible to save Clipboard contents as files if you wish, but the files have still to be opened once the Clipboard contents have gone.

6 Close Recorder if you want to.

7 Make the Accessories group window current in Program Manager and start Write.

8 Maximise Write and use File then Open to retrieve JANE.WRI.

9 Click to position the cursor on a blank line just above PS.

119

■ SECTION 7
Applying the accessories

10 Click Edit then Paste. If Paste is grayed then your macro did not succeed in placing anything on the Clipboard.

The sign off is now slotted into the letter.

Now for some heavy mathematics:

1 Alt-Tab back to Program Manager and open Calculator.

2 Click **1** then **0** three times to put **1000** in the calculator. This step and the next two you might find are quicker if you use the keyboard, rather than the mouse. Simply press the key that corresponds to the key on the calculator.

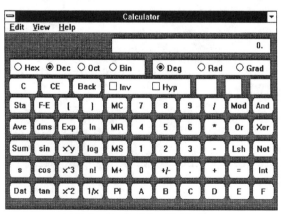

Calcualtor in Scientific Mode

SECTION 7
Applying the accessories

3 Click the plus sign and enter **8000**, in the same way as in step 2.

4 Click the equals sign and the total of 9000 will show on the calculator.

5 Click Edit then Copy. You do not need to highlight calculator entries to place the total of 9000 on the Clipboard.

6 Close Calculator and make Write the current window.

7 Position the cursor just after the £ sign opposite the word *TOTAL*.

8 Click Edit then Paste.

The figure 9000 remains on the Clipboard until you leave Windows or copy or cut new data to it. If you want to check the current contents of Clipboard at any time, open it from the Main group. You may then close it back down. In normal day-to-day operations Clipboard functions quite happily in the background, there is no requirement to have it open to use it. It is not even necessary to have Clipboard showing as an application icon in Program Manager. When you learn how to customise Program Manager you can leave out those applications you rarely open.

■ SECTION 7
Applying the accessories

John Font, the writer of the letter from TypeCast to Rectangle and Circle, is too busy to type in the information about discounts. He decides to paste in the relevant parts of the memo from his MD, Louise. This was created in Notepad and was saved with the filename MEMO.TXT.

1 Open and maximise Notepad. Use Ctrl-Esc or Alt-Tab to switch to Program Manager first.

2 Click File then Open.

3 Open the file MEMO.TXT. You may have to change directories to find the file.

4 Drag the mouse over the section of the memo beginning *As part* and ending with *quoted*.

5 Click Edit followed by Copy.

6 Close Notepad if you want and return to the letter in Write.

■ SECTION 7
Applying the accessories

7 Place the cursor immediately after PS at the end of the letter.

8 Click Edit then Paste. The information about the discount should now be in the letter.

At the moment we are copying and pasting into Write. You are not restricted to pasting into Write. Many of the Windows accessories and Windows applications support pasting. Some go even further than this and support DDE (dynamic data exchange) or *hot links*. The links we have so far created are *cold links*, the clipboarded data is frozen. For example if the costs of publication were to increase and you returned to Calculator and arrived at a new total, then the total that was originally pasted into Write would remain unchanged at £9000. You would have to re-paste the new total into Write. Hot links, by comparison, are always on the boil, as it were. You might have some figures in a Superbase database which you copy to Excel and draw an Excel chart based on the figures. If the data had been transferred via a hot link then any change in the original Superbase data would be reflected in the copy of the data in Excel and the chart would adjust accordingly. DDE is in fact rather more than this, I only wanted to suggest a few ideas.

The next stage is to copy the name and address of Rectangle and Circle into the letter. The name and address are held on an index card in Cardfile in a file called CLIENTS.CRD. By the way, the order in which we are carrying out all this copying and pasting is relatively unimportant. There is no reason why we could not have done the name and address earlier or later.

■ SECTION 7
Applying the accessories

1 Open and maximise Cardfile from the Accessories group window. You might have to use Alt-Tab or Ctrl-Esc to return to Program Manager. And once in Program Manager recall that Ctrl-Tab cycles through the document icons and windows.

2 Click File, Open and open the CLIENTS.CRD file.

3 Click the title of the card for RECTANGLE AND CIRCLE to bring it to the front. There is quite possibly a blank card lying on top of it.

4 Drag the mouse over the text for the name and address on the main body of the card to highlight it.

5 Click Edit, Copy.

6 Close Cardfile if you want and return to Write.

7 Place the cursor in Write immediately above Dear Jane and click Edit, Paste.

SECTION 7
Applying the accessories

The name and address of Rectangle and Circle appears flush with the left margin between the letterhead and the salutation. You might like to insert some blank lines to improve the appearance, press Enter to do so. You can get rid of blank lines with the Backspace key.

The final preparation before the letter is printed and mailed is to incorporate the logo. This is a Paintbrush file with the name LOGO.

1 Cycle to the Program Manager window and open and maximise Paintbrush from the Accessories group window.

2 In Paintbrush click File, Open and choose LOGO.BMP.

3 Click the Pick tool in the Toolbox: the pair of scissors with a dotted rectangle.

4 Place the cursor just to the top left of the logo and drag the mouse to the bottom right of the logo. With the keyboard you hold down the Insert key while using the direction keys. A dotted rectangle is drawn around the logo.

5 Click Edit, Copy and leave Paintbrush if you wish. If you do so, answer No if you are asked to save your changes.

SECTION 7
Applying the accessories

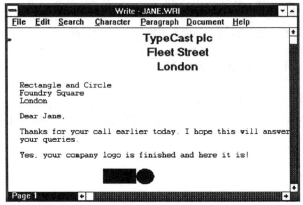

Formatting in Write

6 Return to Write and place the cursor immediately below *and here it is!*

7 Click Edit, Paste to add the logo to the letter.

8 Select the logo in the letter by clicking it. To do this from the keyboard place the cursor at the very top left of the logo and while holding down the Shift key press the Down arrow key.

9 Click Edit, Move Picture and move (do not drag) the logo halfway between the left and right margins and click once. On the keyboard use the Right arrow key and press Enter when it is in position.

SECTION 7
Applying the accessories

0 Your logo has probably become a little distorted with the circle looking more like an ellipse. To rectify this re-select the logo, if necessary, and click Edit, Size Picture. Move the mouse until the proportions seem right and click once. If you are working from the keyboard then pressing the Right arrow first will enable you to stretch or compress the logo horizontally from the right. Left arrow does the same from the left. You can not switch from the left to the right of the logo without going back through Edit, Size Picture.

1 Click File, Save to save the finished letter.

The only thing that remains to do is to print the letter ready for signing by John Font. It can then be mailed or faxed to Rectangle and Circle. In order to print you must have a printer installed to work with Windows. This is done during the Setup installation routine. If your printer is not set up or does not function correctly refer to the section in this book on Control Panel. To print the letter:

1 Click File then Print to see the Print dialogue. This should indicate that only one copy is printed and the check box for Draft quality should not be turned on.

2 Click OK to proceed with printing.

■ SECTION 7
Applying the accessories

3 When you are finished printing close Write.

Until you get to know Windows and your printer, printing can be a little bit tricky. If your printer is supported by Windows and properly installed and configured then printing should take place. You might discover that most of the letter prints on one page with maybe one or two lines on a subsequent page. This looks awful. You can get round this by removing some blank lines from the letter or reducing the font size. You may find that the pound signs (or another currency symbol if you are a non-UK reader) in a letter do not print correctly. There are a number of possible causes for this. One is that incorrect international settings were defined during Setup. They can be altered through Control Panel. The DIP switches on a dot matrix printer may be set incorrectly, you would have to consult your printer manual to solve this. Or you might try changing the font in which the letter is printed. To change the font and/or the font size:

1 Open JANE.WRI. Select the whole of the letter by holding down the Ctrl key as you click in the left margin. To do this from the keyboard press Ctrl-Home to go to the start of the letter and while holding down the Shift key press Ctrl-End.

2 Make any changes through Character, Fonts. Close Write and save your changes if you wish.

The changes, of course, affect all the text in the letter and you need to change the letterhead as we did at the beginning. Otherwise it will remain in the font and font size you have just selected.

PART THREE

Main group and Program Manager

■ SECTION 8
File Manager

File Manager is the housekeeping application and is one of the most powerful and convenient applications bundled with Windows 3. It requires a little patience to learn but is well worth the effort. Once you have used it a few times, say, for copying or deleting files, groups of files, and whole directories, you will begin to wonder why you ever used the DOS prompt for housekeeping. File Manager is originally in the Main group.

File Manager is exactly the same as all other Windows applications in that you can leave it running while working on something else, and switch quickly around applications with Alt-Tab. This is probably a good idea if your work involves a lot of housekeeping, for it saves continually opening and closing File Manager. Advanced users may be interested to realise that you can start Windows with File Manager, rather than Program Manager, as the initial screen. Applications may also be started from File Manager by simply double clicking their names. To start File Manager:

1 In the Main group window double click the File Manager icon.

2 Maximise File Manager by clicking its maximise button. This step is optional though it does give you more room to work in.

A word of warning is in order at this point. File Manager is deceptively powerful. It can show and delete all files, including hidden and system files. It can delete whole directories and sub-directories with all their files in one fell swoop, and can be configured to give no warning at all. Such actions are potentially quite dangerous and traumatic for the user when much valuable

■ SECTION 8
File Manager

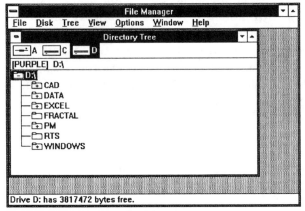

File Manager

work is irretrievably deleted. Until you are completely familiar with File Manager do not alter any settings through Options, Confirmation. Doing so could well result in the suppression of all warning messages, which means you have no opportunity of backing out of accidental actions.

The opening File Manager window has a row of icons along the top representing disk drives on your system. The highlighted icon is the current drive. Your display should display *A:* for your floppy disk drive, and *C:* for the hard disk. In addition you might see *B:* for a second floppy drive and *D:* if your hard disk is partitioned. Those of you who are logged onto a network will see even more drives for *F:* or *G:* and even *X:*, *Y:* and *Z:*. Drive icons representing RAM drives and CD-ROMs are also be displayed if you have them. We are going to concentrate on *A:* and either *C:* or *D:*, depending where you saved the files created so far.

To log onto a different drive simply click the icon for the required drive. If you try to select a floppy drive and no disk is in the drive

SECTION 8
File Manager

you receive an error message. Place a disk in the drive and Retry. The keyboard alternative for logging on to a drive is to type the letter for the drive while holding down the Ctrl key.

The Disk menu option allows you to format, copy or label a disk. There is even an option to format a system disk, that is a bootable floppy disk. The format option will only work with floppy disks so there is no danger of accidentally formatting your hard disk. If you have a high density drive then you can choose between formatting high density and double density disks. The copy option is especially useful for making backup copies of valuable application software disks. If you have not already done so, it might be sensible to backup your original Windows disks as soon as possible. Please note that the original (source) and the copy (destination) disks must have the same capacity for this to work. If they do not, you will need to copy the files through File, Copy or with the mouse. The latter method is covered shortly. You can copy a disk even if you have one floppy disk drive, all you do is follow the instructions on screen about when to switch the source and destination disks in the drive.

The File menu has a range of options. The Copy and Move options are essential if you do not have a mouse. With a mouse it is much easier to copy and move files simply by clicking and dragging. The Delete and Rename selections do just as they indicate, deleting and renaming files. Delete also works on whole directories and disks. Search is useful if you can not remember where you stored a file and wish to retrieve it. Create Directory does just that.

There is also a choice called Open. This is used to open an application once you have selected its main program file in the File Manager window; or you can double click the filename or press Enter on the file. Applications will also start if you double click an associated data file. For example double clicking

SECTION 8
File Manager

JANE.WRI starts Write, with the letter to Jane at Rectangle and Circle already loaded. Windows and Windows applications automatically provide these associations between data file extensions and particular applications. The details are held in a file called WIN.INI. As you become more experienced in Windows you can create your own associations through File, Associate. File Manager is an alternative to Program Manager for starting applications, only the pretty icons and convenient group windows are missing. It is possible in fact to start Windows with File Manager rather than Program Manager as the front end (you would need to alter the shell parameter in a file called SYSTEM.INI).

File Manager is an application window with a Control Menu. As you open directories, to examine or work with their contents, they are displayed in document windows. These document windows have a control menu too, but it is accessed from the keyboard with Alt-Hyphen rather than Alt-Spacebar. Mouse users do not have to worry about such niceties. And remember to cycle document windows with Ctrl-Tab rather than Alt-Tab. The first document window is open and displays the directories on the current drive. The ensuing exercises assume you are logged onto the relevant partition of your hard disk to find the default Windows directory. You should be seeing a list of directories for the current drive, or the root directory only, in the first document window.

To show the root directory only:

1 Place the highlight on the symbol for the root directory. This has a little folder next to it and is labelled *C:* or *D:*. Placing the highlight with the mouse, by clicking the folder symbol is enough. If you highlighted by clicking its label, click the folder symbol. From the keyboard use Tree, Collapse Branch from the menu bar.

■ SECTION 8
File Manager

You will notice a plus sign in the folder. This tells you that there are sub-directories branching from this directory.

2 Click the folder icon to expand the directory tree, be careful not to double click. From the keyboard use Tree, Expand One Level.

The same folder now shows a minus sign. The minus indicates that the directory has sub-directories which are now showing and is collapsible. A plus sign shows an expandable directory. You should see an entry for the Windows directory, you may have to use the scroll bars to find it if you have a lot of directories at this level. The Windows directory folder contains a plus sign.

3 Expand the Windows directory to see the tree of its sub-directories. One of these is called System. You might have one called Temp as well.

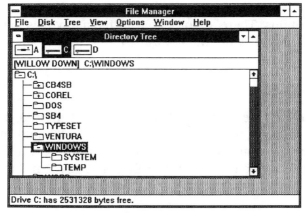

Directory tree

■ SECTION 8
File Manager

4 Collapse the Windows directory to hide the entries for System and Temp.

If at any stage you double click accidentally you will have one or more extra document windows. Close these by double clicking the relevant document Control menus.

Single clicking is for expanding and collapsing a directory tree structure. You see only the names of directories and no files are listed. To see files you have to open a directory. Opening a directory is different from expanding a directory. Opening a directory is accomplished by double rather than single clicking the folder, and opens a document window for the directory. Keyboard users press Enter once the directory has been highlighted with the direction keys. You can open multiple directories at once and Ctrl-Tab through their respective windows. These document windows may also be minimised, re-sized and moved to create as convenient a display as possible.

5 Double click the Windows directory to display the files it contains. There are probably far too many files to fit in the document window, simply use the scroll bars to move around.

6 Find the file called JANE.WRI and highlight it. If you saved your work to a different directory you should close the Windows directory window and open the relevant one. To close a document window from the keyboard press Alt-Hyphen (not Spacebar) and then C for Close.

■ SECTION 8
File Manager

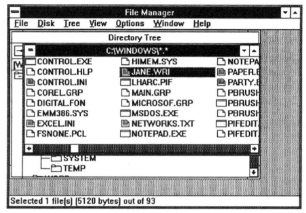

File list

7 Drag the Windows directory document window to one side or down the screen. It should end up in such a position that you can see both the highlighted JANE.WRI file and the icon for drive A.

To complete the next step you will need to place a formatted floppy disk in drive A. If this is not feasible use your hard disk in place of a floppy for the exercise.

8 With the mouse drag from JANE.WRI to the icon for drive A and let go. As you drag you will notice a small symbol. This is a file symbol, and if you highlight and drag multiple files it shows as a multiple file symbol. You can also drag directories around in a similar manner. You then have to respond to one or more confirmation messages (or possibly none at all, this depends upon any previous settings through Options, Confirmation). Answer in the affirmative

■ SECTION 8
File Manager

and JANE.WRI is copied to drive A. If you do not have a floppy, drag to the symbol for the root directory of the hard disk.

When you drag from one drive to another the file is copied. You can force Windows to move the file, that is copy it first and then delete the original, by pressing the Alt key as you drag. When you drag a file to a new destination on the same disk it is automatically moved. In this case, to leave the original intact, you must force Windows to copy rather than move. This is done by holding down the Ctrl key as you drag.

Keyboard users have to choose File then Copy or Move after highlighting the file.

The previous operation is on a single file. The procedure is the same when working on a single directory. You can also work with multiple files or directories at the same time. In order to do so you must first make a multiple selection. There are various ways of doing this, it depends upon whether the files are next to each other (contiguous) or scattered throughout the directory window (non-contiguous).

> To select a contiguous group of files (for example to copy multiple files in one go) click the first one and, while holding down the Shift key, click the last file in the group. Keyboard users need to use direction keys instead of dragging. To select a non-contiguous group of files hold down the Ctrl key as you click each required file. From the keyboard press and release Shift-F8, press the spacebar for each required file and press Shift-F8 again to finish. By combining the techniques for contiguous and non-contiguous groups you can select non-contiguous groups of contiguous files, if you see what I mean. I will leave you to practice this in the

SECTION 8
File Manager

Windows directory, though please do not do anything with them. A shortcut for selecting all the files in a document window is to press Ctrl-Forward Slash (/) or File, Select All.

For the final exercise in File Manager try and locate two or more of the following files in the Windows directory window: LOGO.BMP, MEMO.TXT, CLIENTS.CRD, RECT.CAL, SIGNOFF.REC.

9 Select two or more of these files (do not select JANE.WRI which will be required in a later exercise.) Make very sure that is all you have selected.

0 Click File then Delete.

1 Click the Delete button in the subsequent dialogue. Choose Cancel if you have any doubts about the wisdom of your action.

2 If a confirmation message appears click Yes. Choose No if doubts have just crept in, we do not want to delete files that are vital to the operation of Windows.

If you did happen to delete important program files you have to install Windows again, unless you have some kind of undelete utility. Perhaps that is the only thing missing from File Manager, an option that allows you to undo deletions of files.

■ SECTION 8
File Manager

13 Close File Manager by double clicking its application window Control menu.

In the subsequent dialogue make sure the Save Settings check box is turned off before clicking OK.

SECTION 9
Program Manager

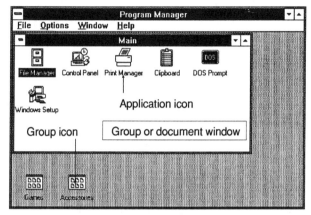

Program Manager

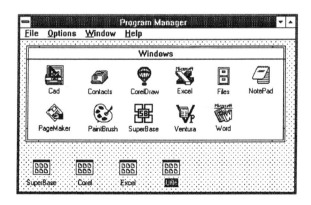

Customised Program Manager

SECTION 9
Program Manager

This book has taken us straight from the installation of Windows to this point by accepting the Windows defaults. Thus we have been working with accessories, and other applications and utilities from the accessories and main groups. There is no reason why you should not customise Program Manager to your own tastes. For example you might want to remove the Clipboard icon (this will not prevent you from copying and pasting). PIF Editor is probably not required. If you use Notepad and File Manager a lot, you might like to keep them in the same group window. You might want to have your application icons for separately purchased applications in the same group as Paintbrush. Solitaire might prove so much of a distraction that you get no work done, and want to remove the games group. You might not like the name *main* for a group, or want to change the name Paintbrush to Graphics, or you might wish to rearrange the layout of icons within a group window. All of this and more can be configured from Program Manager. When you exit from Windows and turn on the Save Changes check box, in the Exit Windows dialogue, Program Manager remembers the latest settings and starts up exactly how you left it. Should you be pleased with the new layout turn off Save Changes, so that any further accidental changes are forgotten.

It is important to realise that exercises in this section alter the way Windows looks. Should this not be what you want then read the section as a reference, and do not follow through the practical steps. You should then be in a position to put Windows back together, as it was originally. Though if you are going to use Windows on a day-to-day basis you will invariably want to customise Program Manager. This section looks at some of the options available.

SECTION 9
Program Manager

To rename a group:

1 Minimise the Main group, if it is a window, into an icon. Select the icon by clicking or with Ctrl-Tab.

2 Click File then Properties.

3 Type **Utilities** to replace Main in the text box and click OK.

To create a brand new group:

1 Click File then New to summon the New Program Object dialogue.

2 In this dialogue choose the Program Group option button and click OK. The next dialogue is called Program Group Properties.

3 In the text box labelled Description type **Mine** and click OK. Leave the Group File text box empty, Windows automatically creates a file called MINE.GRP to describe the new group window.

■ SECTION 9
Program Manager

The new group window is the same as the ones we have been working with up till now. It may be minimised, moved and sized. It does not yet contain any icons, we will see how to place icons into group windows later.

To delete a group, make the Mine group current as an icon or window and click File, Delete, and respond in the affirmative to the warning message. If the group contains application icons then you should minimise the group first, otherwise the deletion applies only to the currently highlighted program icon and not to the group as a whole.

To place a brand new application icon in a group:

1 Make the Utilities group current.

2 Click File then New.

3 In the New Program Object dialogue choose the option button for Program Item (not Program Group) and click OK.

4 The Program Item Properties dialogue appears. In the Description text box type **Second Paintbrush**.

■ SECTION 9
Program Manager

5 Press the Tab key or click to move to the Command Line text box and type **PBRUSH**.

You must enter the name of the main program file in the Command Line box. If the program is not in a directory on the DOS path, or in the Windows directory, you must enter its full path-name – for example C:\WINDOWS\PBRUSH. If you follow the program name by a space and then the filename for a data file, associated with that program, the icon starts the program with the data file already loaded.

6 Click OK and maximise the Utilities window, if necessary, to see the icon for Second Paintbrush.

To delete an application icon:

1 Make sure that the Utilities window is open and the Second Paintbrush icon is selected.

2 Click File then Delete and click Yes in the warning message.

The above method for adding an application icon is the one to adopt for adding brand new application icons (you can also use Setup from Utilities in the main group, or drag a filename from File Manager into Program Manager). If an icon is already there, in another group, it is easier to drag the icon from one group to another. As you drag you will either copy or move the icon. You can in fact make copies of the same icon in the same group. To

■ SECTION 9
Program Manager

copy, rather than move, hold down the Ctrl key as you drag the icon. To move an icon:

1 Have both the Accessories and the Utilities group windows open. Move and size both these windows so that you can see the contents of both. Maximising Program Manager itself gives you that little bit more room.

2 Drag the File Manager from the Utilities group into the Accessories group and let go of the mouse button. The keyboard alternative is to highlight the icon, choose File, Move, and select the name of the destination group.

The icons may be repositioned by dragging them, individually, within the group window. Or you might wish to tidy them up in one go. To rearrange the icons in a group window:

1 Make sure the Accessories group window is both open and current.

2 Click Window on the Program Manager menu bar and then Arrange icons.

If you are not keen on the changes, drag File Manager back into the Utilities window, and rename Utilities back to Main. Should you prefer to keep the name Utilities remember that any future references to Main refer to Utilities. This would also apply if you were to go back and repeat earlier sections of this book.

SECTION 10
Print Manager

Print Manager is a bit like Clipboard in that it normally works away quite happily in the background. You can afford to ignore it most of time, unless you wish to interrupt the printing process or change the order in which multiple files are printed.

Only Windows accessories and Windows-based applications work with Print Manager. Any standard application run from Windows by-passes the Print Manager and writes directly to the printer. Windows software follows a more circuitous route when printing. The file to be printed is sent from the application to Windows which assigns the print file to the control of Print Manager. Print Manager in turn channels the file to the printer. This all sounds a little complicated. In fact it one of the great strengths of Windows. It means that Windows handles all the printing, and applications are easier to install. With standard applications, each one has to be separately configured to work with your printer and involves specifying the correct printer driver each time. With Windows you need only do this once, when you install Windows – or if you change your printer later you use Control Panel. Windows takes care of all drivers, whether for printers or monitors, and applications are free to concentrate on what they are best at, processing data. And once the file has been passed to Print Manager, which is essentially a printing application, you can go on working – there is no need to wait for printing to finish. Even if you are waiting for the application to hand the file over to Print Manager you can always Alt-Tab to another application, no more sitting around watching the printer.

Print Manager is installed during Setup, by leaving the Print Manager check box turned on during the printer installation routine. If for any reason you turned this off it may be turned on again through the Printers icon in Control Panel. Without Print Manager, applications write directly to the printer, or the network

■ SECTION 10
Print Manager

printer queue. However you can not carry on with other work until this is finished.

When you print locally Print Manager appears automatically as an icon at the foot of the screen. If you print remotely, that is across a network, the icon does not appear. The way to take a look at Print Manager depends upon whether you are on a network or not. If you are printing to your own dedicated printer, attached locally to your computer, double click the Print Manager icon at the bottom of the screen. This icon disappears when printing finishes, so you have to be quick if you are printing a small file. If you are on a network then you must double click the Print Manager application icon in the Main group. The README.TXT file in the main Windows directory contains valuable information and is worth printing out. This, incidentally, applies to all the TXT files that Setup copied into your Windows directory. To take a look at Print Manager:

1 Open Notepad from the Accessories group.

2 In Notepad click File, Open.

3 Choose the README.TXT file in your Windows directory.

4 Click File, Print.

■ SECTION 10
Print Manager

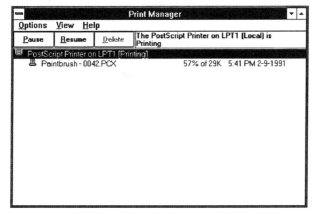

Print Manager

5 Double click the Print Manager icon. This is the one at the foot of the screen if you are printing locally. Those of you on a network should double click the icon in the Main group. In either case you might have to do some Alt-Tabbing first to expose the icon.

6 When you have had a look, minimise the Print Manager window if you are printing locally or close it if you are on a network.

7 Close Notepad.

The Print Manager window gives you the status of your printers and current print jobs. It also enables you to control the print jobs. The list of files waiting to be printed is called a print queue.

■ SECTION 10
Print Manager

You can change the order of the queue if there is something urgent; interrupt, resume and cancel printing. There is, in addition, an option to control the speed of printing.

- To interrupt printing, click the Pause button.

- To resume printing after an interruption, click the Resume button.

- To cancel printing an individual file, select the file from the print queue list and click Delete.

- To cancel printing all files in the queue, click Options then Exit.

- To change the order of files in the print queue drag the filename to its new position in the print queue. From the keyboard you hold down the Ctrl key while using Up and Down arrow keys.

- To change the speed of printing, click Options followed by Low, Medium or High Priority. The High Priority option dedicates more processor time to printing. This speeds up printing but other activities run slower. This is fine if you are happy to wait for printing to finish and have no desire to multi-task. Medium Priority is the default setting and is the best choice for normal work with Windows.

Please note that you are not able to change the print queue order if you are printing across a network. On some networks you may not be allowed to interrupt and resume printing. If you delete one or more files from a print queue you may have to turn your printer off and back on again to flush the printer's buffer.

■ SECTION 11
Control Panel

Control Panel is one of the application icons in the Main group window. Starting Control Panel displays the Control Panel window. This window itself contains a set of icons. The number of icons shown is determined by your particular hardware configuration, but there will be either ten, eleven or twelve icons. The first ten icons are standard. There is an additional icon if you are on a network or running Windows in enhanced mode. If you are in both enhanced mode *and* on a network there are two extra icons. Possibly the most important and most widely used of the icons is the one for Printers. This is not to be confused with Print Manager. Printers allows you to add printers and configure printers for use with Windows. Print Manager allows you to control actual printing. Some of the other icons you hardly, if ever, need to use. We will mention the role of the various icons only briefly, apart from Printers which can be quite important. Any readers interested in more details about the other icons are referred to the Windows User's Guide.

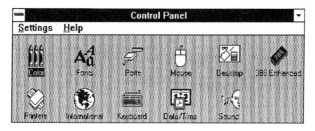

Control Panel

Color

You may have already met this one as you worked through the book. It gives access to a range of colour schemes for Windows should you get bored with the default colours, though the icon is of little use if your monitor is monochrome. When you are bored

151

SECTION 11
Control Panel

with the colour schemes on offer you can always create your own. Double clicking the Color icon summons the Color dialogue box. This is where you choose the colour scheme, through the Color Schemes drop-down list box. If you want to alter the existing schemes then click the Color Palette button. This button has a double chevron which means it extends the present dialogue. The expanded dialogue reveals another button labelled Define Custom Colors. Use this button to alter the range of colours available for the colour schemes.

Printers

This icon is essential if you want to tell Windows about a new printer. If you do not tell Windows, you will not be able to use that printer properly with Windows or Windows-based applications. Printers is valuable too, if you wish to remove a printer or change the way your printer is configured.

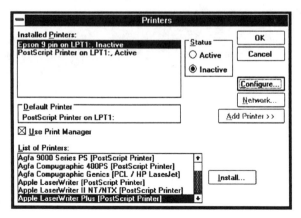

Printer Setup dialogue

■ SECTION 11
Control Panel

Double clicking the Printers icon opens the Printers dialogue. The following information is almost identical to the detailed printer installation instructions in the section: Installing Windows 3. In the Printers dialogue is a check box Print Manager. Make sure the check box is selected, which is the default.

Click the Add Printer button. There are now two main list boxes in the dialogue. The top one is where previously chosen printer/s are listed. The lower one contains available printers. To see the lower list you have to click Add Printer first. This step is only necessary if you wish to add a new printer. The Configure button is sufficient for altering the setup for an existing printer. You can scroll through the lower list by clicking the up and down arrows on the vertical scroll bar. Pressing Page Up or Page Down keys jumps quickly through the list.

Find your new printer in the list of available printers. If your printer is not listed find one with which your printer is compatible. You may have to consult your printer manual to discover compatible printers.

In the rare event that your printer or a compatible printer is not shown in the list you should try choosing the Generic / Text Only option, and ask your dealer for a Windows 3 driver for your particular printer. While you are waiting for the driver to arrive you should be able to print text, albeit of suspect quality. The driver for your printer can always be installed later by choosing Unlisted Printer.

Select the relevant printer to add by clicking its name, then click the Install button. You will be asked to insert one of the Windows disks. Do so and click OK.

SECTION 11
Control Panel

The name of the printer appears in the top list of installed printers. There are one or two other things that Windows needs to know about your printer. You must specify the port to which your printer is attached, usually LPT1 which is the main parallel port. And depending on your particular printer, you can set such parameters as paper size, printing resolution and page orientation. If you are in any doubt over the parameters you can try US Letter or A4 for paper size, the highest resolution for printing and portrait orientation for the page. Laser printers have more options, for example for font cartridges. Your dealer may be able to give advice if you are unsure of the correct choices. Windows will also ask for something called Timeouts. Accept the defaults presented when this happens.

With the name of the installed printer highlighted in the list box at the top of the dialogue click the Configure button to see the Printer Configure dialogue. Highlight the relevant port for your printer and accept the Timeouts defaults by clicking Setup.

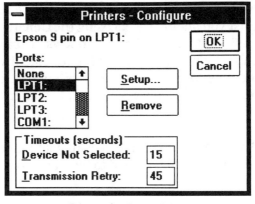

Printers Configure dialogue

SECTION 11
Control Panel

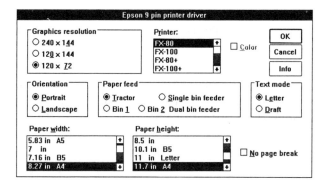

Printer specific dialogue

Next dialogue differs from printer to printer. The title of the dialogue reflects the printer currently being configured and is where you set paper size and so on. It is impossible to give much guidance here as the settings depend upon the individual user and printer. Make the choices that seem appropriate or accept the defaults.

You will see a list box called Printer. This is actually a drop-down list and is accessed by clicking the down arrow to the right. Keyboard users would need to press the Down arrow key while holding down the Alt key. This drop-down list allows you to specify more exactly the type of printer and is worth investigating. Click OK when you are satisfied with your settings.

You are returned to the Printers Configure dialogue.

Click OK in the Printers Configure dialogue to go back to the Printers dialogue.

155

■ SECTION 11
Control Panel

You can repeat these actions for additional printers should you wish. The final stage in configuring a printer is to check it is the active printer. This is only necessary if you install more than one printer.

If you have more than one printer in the list of installed printers at the top of the Printers dialogue, highlight your main printer and click the Active option button.

You can then click OK to exit from Printers.

Fonts

This option is normally accessed only if you buy extra fonts for your printer or for the screen. Understanding fonts and how they work is probably one of the more difficult aspects of Windows. Having said that, adding fonts is straightforward. Double clicking the Fonts icon brings forth the Fonts dialogue. Click the Add button, select the filename for the font and click OK. To remove

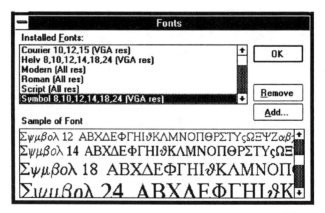

Fonts dialogue

SECTION 11
Control Panel

unwanted fonts click the Remove button. Be careful not to remove the Helv font which is the one used by Windows for dialogue box text. Going into Fonts is a handy way of viewing your fonts. Click the font name in the Installed Fonts list box and you see a sample of the font in various point sizes in the Sample of Font box.

International

This icon is for changing those parameters that are likely to differ from country to country. These parameters include formats for dates, times, currency and numbers, and units of measurement. The first three settings in the International dialogue box are labelled Country, Language and Keyboard Layout. Although they might sound as if they do pretty much the same thing, they are in fact different. Changing Country changes many options to reflect conventions in the particular country, for example the Date Format might change, the Currency Format almost certainly will. Language governs the way in which applications carry out sorting

International dialogue

■ SECTION 11
Control Panel

and case conversion. Keyboard Layout varies special characters and symbols normally available on the keyboard.

Ports

Ports applies to your serial ports only and has no effect at all on the parallel port. The parallel port (LPT1 for instance) is the one to which most of us connect our printer. Serial ports (COM1 for instance) are frequently the connections for modems, some mice and occasionally printers. If you wish to use a modem, for example, possibly with Terminal, then you should set the parameters for the serial port through Ports. You can also alter the settings from Terminal itself. A typical parameter that needs specifying is the speed at which data is transmitted through the port, called the baud rate.

Keyboard

This icon has one purpose only, to adjust the rate at which a keystroke is repeated if you hold the key down. The Keyboard dialogue has a scroll bar where you drag the scroll box anywhere from Slow to Fast. The Test Typematic box in the dialogue is for testing the Repeat Rate setting.

Mouse

This icon is essential if you are left-handed and invaluable if you are having trouble double clicking. The Mouse dialogue includes a check box which, if turned on, reverses the left and right mouse buttons. When selected the index finger of the left hand resting on the right button can be used for normal clicking and double clicking. The Double Click Speed scroll bar is to adjust the speed at which you must double click. If you experience any problems in double clicking quickly enough, drag the scroll box towards the

SECTION 11
Control Panel

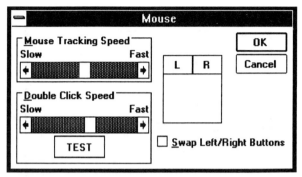

Mouse dialogue

Slow end of the scroll bar. You can try out the new speed by double clicking the Test button. This is highlighted if your double click is successful. The scroll bar for Mouse Tracking Speed dictates responsiveness of mouse pointer to mouse movements. A Slow mouse tracking speed makes for a very lazy pointer. A Fast speed gives the pointer the appearance of being hyperactive.

Date/Time

This is for resetting system date and time. First you select the element of time or date that you wish to modify, for example day or minute and type in the correct number. Or you can select then click the arrows to wind backwards or forwards.

Desktop

Unless you have already been into Desktop, the background behind open windows and icons is rather plain. The background is best seen by closing all accessories and applications and minimising Program Manager.

■ SECTION 11
Control Panel

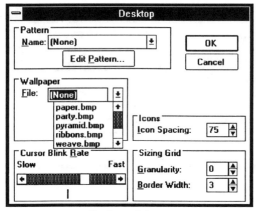

Desktop dialogue

Desktop provides some alternatives. In the Desktop dialogue, Pattern allows you to choose from a range of patterns for the background. Wallpaper allows you to display a bit-mapped (BMP) graphic on the background. Some of those provided cover all the background, others are too small for this. The latter can be reproduced to cover the whole screen by turning on the Tile option button. Front cover of this book shows a screen shot of Windows 3. In the background is a chess board with some flying chess pieces. This is a full screen wallpaper and is called CHESS.BMP. In the Paintbrush window of the screen shot is the PAPER.BMP. If you like you can create your own wallpaper in Paintbrush save it as BMP not PCX and type its name in the Wallpaper File text box. If the bit-mapped file is not stored in the Windows directory you have to specify its full path-name. Bit-mapped wallpapers require large amounts of memory in order to display, so if memory is at a premium do not wallpaper Windows.

The Cursor Blink Rate section does exactly as it says, complete with a little demonstration underneath. The Icons section enables

SECTION 11
Control Panel

you to alter the space between icons in group windows. This is especially handy if icon descriptions tend to overlap. You could of course always shorten descriptions (see the section on Program Manager). The Sizing Grid section of the dialogue contains defaults for two parameters. Granularity determines layout of the invisible grid that lies behind Program Manager. A setting of 0 indicates that the grid is not in effect. Any positive number creates a grid, and windows and icons snap to this grid. An entry of 1 sets an eight pixel grid, 2 a sixteen pixel grid and so on. Grids keep icons and windows neatly aligned. Border Width alters the width of borders around windows – this is only true for windows that can be resized.

Sound

Absence of an undelete utility and this feature are the only disappointing aspects of Windows 3. I was totally misled by the musical notes floating next to the head in the Sound icon. I thought it might provide a Midi interface emulator and let me compose great music on my keyboard. Alas, no! Sound turns the warning beep on or off – that's all.

Network

This icon is only be visible if you are on a network. The exact nature of options available by double clicking the icon varies from network to network. You might be able to do such things as sign on or off the network, send messages across the network or alter your network password.

386 Enhanced

Presently only a few readers are likely to see this icon: it only displays if you have a 386 machine with a minimum of two

SECTION 11
Control Panel

megabytes of RAM. Hopefully in a couple of years time all of us may see it, as people upgrade their hardware. Even then, however, it is doubtful if you will ever need to use it. It is there to configure defaults for device contention and scheduling of multi-tasking. In the vast majority of cases the defaults originally set by Windows are perfectly adequate. Should you have cause to change any of the defaults, then you are probably in a situation where you know what you are doing anyway, and you are referred to the section on Control Panel and the chapter on More About Applications in the Windows User's Guide.

■ SECTION 12
Clipboard

Most of the time Clipboard works invisibly in the background. Whenever you choose either Copy or Cut in the Edit menu of accessories and applications data is placed automatically on the clipboard. Copying data leaves the original data intact while cutting data removes it. In order to copy or cut data it must be selected first. Depending upon the nature of the source and destination application you may transfer text or graphics or both. To insert the data from the clipboard into the destination application (this can be in fact the source application) position the cursor and click Edit, Paste. If Paste is grayed then there is no data on the clipboard. Clipboard data remains in place until it is overwritten with a subsequent cut or copy, or is cleared with Edit, Delete in the Cilpboard menu, or you exit Windows.

Once data is held on the Clipboard it is possible to paste it as many times as you wish. To view the current contents of the Clipboard double click its icon in the Main group window. In some applications Clipboard is an option in the application's Control menu. This data may be saved directly from Clipboard with File, Save and retrieved in a later session with File, Open. The data is saved in a file with a CLP extension. Saved data is particularly useful if you paste the same data from session to session, for example a company logo, as it obviates the need to copy or cut in every session.

Clipboard can be cleared at any time through Edit, Delete. You may capture screen-shots to Clipboard where they are held in BMP format. If your application supports BMP files then you can paste the screen-shot directly. Otherwise you will have to paste into Paintbrush, which supports BMP, and save out in PCX format which is recognised by numerous applications. The Print Screen key captures the entire screen, Alt-Print Screen the active window.

SECTION 13
DOS Icon

The DOS icon in the Main group returns you to the DOS prompt. It does not however exit Windows and you can return immediately to Windows by typing EXIT. You can switch easily from the DOS prompt to other applications with Alt-Tab. If you are running in Windows enhanced mode then the DOS prompt can be seen in a window as well as full screen. To switch from full screen to a window press Alt-Enter and the same to switch back. Again if you are in enhanced mode, this DOS prompt may be configured to actually start up in a window. Most Windows users should never have recourse to this DOS prompt. However should you like to try it anyway, do not run the DOS CHKDSK utility. If the latter is your intention, you might be worried by a disk problem, then quit Windows altogether before you do so.

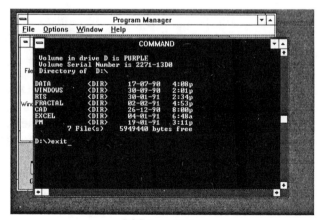

DOS in a window

■ SECTION 14
Windows Setup

When you update or alter your hardware in any way Windows needs to be aware of the new system. Fortunately it is rarely necessary to go through the whole installation routine. Addition of a new printer or set of fonts is handled by Control Panel. The Windows Setup icon is there if you change your display, keyboard, mouse or network (or you add a mouse or are connected to a network for the first time). Settings may be changed by clicking Options then Change System Settings in the Windows Setup dialogue. The Change System Settings dialogue is very similar to what you see during initial installation of Windows. When you do make alterations to the settings you are asked to restart Windows or reboot the machine, and you click the suggested button.

There is also an option to add new applications to your group windows. This functions in exactly the same manner as it does during installation of Windows. You will probably find it much more convenient to add applications in Program Manager, and you are advised to re-read the section on Program Manager as and when you purchase new applications for your computer.

	Windows Setup
Options Help	
Display:	VGA with Monochrome display
Keyboard:	Enhanced 101 or 102 key US and Non US
Mouse:	Microsoft, or IBM PS/2
Network:	Network not installed
Swap file:	Permanent (4098 K bytes on Drive C:)

Windows setup dialogue

PART FOUR

A closer look at Accessories

■ SECTION 15
More on accessories

All accessories are covered in depth in the Windows User's Guide and each one has Help on the menu bar. Given those references and the practical introduction earlier in this book, the accessories should present few problems. The Windows accessories that you turn to most often will, of course, depend upon the nature of your work. It is likely, however, that most users, in the absence of any separately purchased applications, use mainly Write, Cardfile, and perhaps Paintbrush. The next three sections take a closer look at these particular accessories.

■ SECTION 16
Cardfile

Cardfile is a flat-file database and is suitable for holding records in an index card manner. You can have as many index card files as you wish and open two or more at the same time. What you may not do is to easily relate the files together, (for that a full-blown relational database like Superbase is necessary), although you could bodge your way around this with a suitable Recorder macro, but that is quite difficult and complex. Let us return to TypeCast by way of example. TypeCast has a client called Rectangle and Circle for whom it has designed a logo. As a consequence Rectangle and Circle owes TypeCast a sum of money. In a file for clients TypeCast enters a balance outstanding on the record for Rectangle and Circle. But suppose Rectangle and Circle supplies TypeCast with paper and TypeCast owes some money for this. In a file for suppliers TypeCast enters its balance outstanding on the record for Rectangle and Circle. When TypeCast draws up its accounts it may wish to ascertain its overall balance with Rectangle and Circle. This is simply a matter of calculating the difference between what it owes and what it is owed. A relational database would find matching records in both files and extract the necessary data automatically. In Cardfile this would have to be done manually by moving to the matching records in each file separately, and doing the calculation of the overall balance in Calculator.

Nonetheless Cardfile is a valuable accessory and is ideal for storing lists of names and addresses, catalogues and so on. The following exercise demonstrates some of the facilities available within Cardfile.

1 Open and maximise Cardfile. If you habitually open the same file in Cardfile you can instruct Cardfile to open the file automatically. There are many ways of doing so. One method is to use File, Properties in Program Manager and

■ SECTION 16
Cardfile

append the name of the file to the Command Line entry for Cardfile. Another involves creation of separate icons for the most popular Cardfile files, through File, New in Program Manager.

A new file displays as a single blank index card. The cursor is positioned ready in the information area of the card. Above the information area is a double line and above that is the index line. Text entered in the index line is used as a basis for sorting the cards, you might like to think of it as the key field. The status line immediately below the menu bar indicates which view is current, whether Card View or List View. To the right of this are a couple of scroll arrows for moving through a stack of cards or a list – Cardfile does not have scroll bars. Finally there is a count of the total number of cards (records) in the file.

The initial step in creating a new file is to enter the data for each record. This is a two-stage process. First the index or key field is typed in the index line then the rest of the data (or fields) is typed into the information area.

2 Click Card followed by Add. For the first card only you can also click Edit followed by Index or double click the index line.

3 Type the key field data **RECTANGLE AND CIRCLE**, in the subsequent Add (or Index) dialogue and click OK.

Clicking OK puts the cursor back in the information area. You then have a choice. You can either enter all the data for that record or move on to the key field for the next cards. For the latter you

171

■ SECTION 16
Cardfile

repeat steps 2 and 3 for each card in turn then go back to type in the information area for every card.

4 Type the following in the information area:

> **Rectangle and Circle**
> **Foundry Square**
> **London**

5 Repeat steps 2 to 4 for about twenty cards.

We do not want this to turn into a typing exercise so you could leave the information areas blank and simply enter one letter of the alphabet in the index line. Make this a different letter for each card and do not follow alphabetical order. Alternatively you might wish to record real data for your own name and address file, you can always delete Rectangle and Circle later.

Whatever your entries, they are displayed in alphabetical or numeric order. If you have both numeric and alphabetic index lines the numeric ones are sorted first. Should you be using two digit numbers make sure that you have 01 and not 1, similarly for three digit numbers, 001, 002 not 1,2. If you want a particular card to be first in the stack, perhaps called NOTES, type a space before the name. The card first in the stack always shows at the front when you open Cardfile. Of course, although the cards always stay in order, it is possible to have any card as the front card. The first card is then somewhere else in the stack, but the

SECTION 16
Cardfile

order is still maintained. If you can see an A in the middle of the stack it will be preceded by Z and followed by a B then a C, assuming you entered these letters.

6 Make sure RECTANGLE AND CIRCLE is not at the front. If necessary click any other index line to bring that card to the front.

7 Bring RECTANGLE AND CIRCLE to the front, bring any other card to the front and once more get RECTANGLE AND CIRCLE. There are lots of ways of doing this and you might wish to try one or more of them. The list indicates the various options for moving through a stack of cards.

- If you can see the card, click its index line.

- If the card has disappeared off the top of the screen, click a card near the back to move the whole stack forward. Repeat this until the card comes into view then click its index line.

- Click Search then Go To. Type one or more letters in the text box and click OK. You must type enough letters to distinguish the index line from any others. For example if you had an R as well as RECTANGLE AND CIRCLE then you type **RE** (or re or Re or rE). Typing **R** brings that card to the front and RECTANGLE AND CIRCLE is not far away.

■ SECTION 16
Cardfile

- Click Search then Find. Type **FOUNDRY** (or even FO) in the text box and click OK. Go To searches index lines while Find searches information areas. Find Next repeats the previous Find.

- Click the scroll arrows on the status line until the card comes to the front.

- Press Page Up and Page Down keys to scroll card by card backwards and forwards (Ctrl-Home gets the first card, Ctrl-End the final card).

- Press Ctrl-R to bring the first R to the front, then scroll card by card. This works in both Card and List View.

- Click View followed by List. In List View you may see scroll bars. Use the scroll bars to move through the list of cards and click *RECTANGLE AND CIRCLE*. Click View followed by Card.

- Press Alt-V then L to switch to List View. Use Page Up or Page Down keys to jump through the list. Press the Down arrow (or Right arrow) to move one card forward. Backward is Up arrow (or Left arrow). Highlight *RECTANGLE AND CIRCLE* and press Alt-V then C to return to Card View.

8 Change the index entry for *RECTANGLE AND CIRCLE* to *WEIRD NON-EUCLIDEAN THINGS*. Bring the card to the front and double click its index line. Or you could try Edit, Index. If you are in List View double clicking has the same effect.

SECTION 16
Cardfile

9 Change the data in the information area from *Rectangle and Circle* to *Weird Non-Euclidean Things*. Bring the card to the front and click the appropriate part of the information area. If text to be altered is on the first line then the cursor is in position. By deleting and inserting text, change *Rectangle and Circle* to *Weird Non-Euclidean Things*. Remember the quickest way to delete a contiguous block of text is to select it by dragging and then press the Delete key. The new company name *Weird Non-Euclidean Things* is just asking for a new logo – more on this later.

0 Print the card by clicking File then Print. If you want to print all the cards click Print All rather than Print.

1 Make a copy of the card by clicking Card, Duplicate. Change some of the text in the duplicate to make it slightly different from the original. Duplication is handy if two cards contain similar information.

Or you can try Edit, Copy to place selected text on the Clipboard and then Edit, Paste with another card at the front. Edit, Cut removes selected data from the current card. This followed by Edit, Paste on another card is the equivalent of moving, rather than copying, data from one card to another.

2 Delete the amended duplicate by clicking Card, Delete and answering OK to the warning message.

■ SECTION 16
Cardfile

13 Make sure that the card for *WEIRD NON-EUCLIDEAN THINGS* is at the front and change the line for London to Tirana.

14 Click Edit then Restore to undo the change. Note that Edit, Restore goes back to the last saved version of a card, but it does not work if you bring any other card to the front in the meantime. Edit, Restore is suitable for undoing multiple changes to a card. Edit, Undo undoes the last change only. Edit, Undo is a toggle, and with it you may undo the previous undo.

15 Add an extra line to the information area. Type 071–111–1111 on this line.

16 Click Card followed by Autodial. Cardfile automatically places the first number it finds in the information area into the Autodial dialogue. To avoid confusion with street numbers or numeric post codes, you must place the telephone number on the first line of a card's information area.

For the Autodial facility to work you need a Hayes-compatible modem connected to one of the serial ports on your computer, and a valid telephone number on the card. You could enter a commonly used prefix, for instance a 9 to access an outside line, in the Prefix text box. To incorporate the prefix turn on the Use Prefix check box. The Setup button expands the Autodial dialogue. In the expanded dialogue you can set the correct port for the modem, specify the baud rate and switch between tone and pulse telephone lines.

■ SECTION 16
Cardfile

17 Click Cancel to exit the Autodial dialogue. Clicking OK initiates the telephone call.

18 Click File then Save to keep the index file, it is needed in a later exercise. Enter **CUSTOMER** as the filename and click OK.

19 Close Cardfile.

The previous nineteen steps demonstrate most of the features of Cardfile. It is quite a versatile accessory and often gets overlooked by Windows users. Apart from some generic menu options, that is options appearing on most windows' menu bars, the only things not considered are the File, Merge option, and Picture and Text in the Edit menu. The latter two are covered in due course. File, Merge is for consolidating two or more index card files. One of the files must be open and the consolidated set adopts its name if you use File Save. File, Save As allows you to enter a new name for the merged files. The second file is left intact and you may wish to delete this file through File Manager. To add a third file you repeat the whole process, with the first merged file as the current file.

■ SECTION 17
Paintbrush

The fact that Rectangle and Circle has changed its name to Weird Non-Euclidean Things is a perfect excuse for designing a new logo. The name would suggest some kind of free-form, stream-of-consciousness artwork. With Paintbrush a step-by-step practical exercise needs a book in itself if we were to cover all the options. The options are discussed anyway in the Windows User's Guide. Probably the best way to learn Paintbrush is to experiment, the new logo is an ideal opportunity. This section mentions some of the options and it is up to you to try them out as you read. If you share my lack of artistic ability you may end up with a mess, but that is precisely what is required for the new logo.

To begin you open Paintbrush, of course, and to end choose File, Save and enter the filename **WEIRD**. In between feel free to slap paint all over the place.

Paintbrush saves files with a BMP extension. This is a fairly recent file format and may not yet be supported by some Windows-based applications. If you choose File, Save for the first time or File, Save As you will notice an Options button. Clicking this button expands the File Save As dialogue then you can click the option button for PCX. PCX is a long established file format and is usually supported by other applications. Should you have fully-compatible versions of Windows applications the PCX option is probably not necessary. Some readers may have graphics files created with earlier releases of Windows in an accessory called Paint. These have the MSP file extension. You can load these into Paintbrush, though they are saved back out with the BMP (or PCX if you select it) extension. To open a Paint MSP file first click File, Open. The Open From section of the ensuing dialogue should be defaulting to BMP. Click the MSP option button instead. Note the PCX option as well, should you work with PCX files.

SECTION 17
Paintbrush

When Paintbrush opens the Brush tool is selected. Dragging the mouse across the drawing area leaves a streak of paint.

1 Try painting a few doodles.

There are various parameters that affect the appearance of your painting. The Linesize box can be utilised to work with a fatter or thinner brush. Just click the desired thickness. The foreground colour or pattern is the one used by the brush. Clicking Options followed by Brush Shapes allows you to change the type of brush. Some of the brush shapes result in delicate calligraphic effects, or not so delicate!

2 Paint a few more doodles, but work with differing linesizes, foreground colours and brush shapes.

3 The Airbrush tool is for spraying drops of paint. A light airbrushing can produce subtle shading effects. Heavy airbrushing, that is dragging repeatedly over the same area, gives a denser appearance. The airbrush really demands a variation on dragging, something I call wiggling the mouse. Wiggling involves holding down the mouse button and shaking the mouse from side to side. You will see what I mean when you try it. Spray a few lighter and denser patches of paint. Change the foreground colour and linesize to provide some variation.

■ SECTION 17
Paintbrush

4 Go back to the Brush tool and paint an enclosed area, such as a wobbly polygon. The inside of the area is in the background colour and the outline in the current foreground colour.

5 Change the foreground colour in the Palette and click the Paint Roller tool.

6 Place the tip of the paint roller inside the enclosed area and click. You may also roll paint over lines. Try clicking the tip of the roller on a line, and the line takes on the current foreground colour. If you miss the line, or an enclosed area for that matter, paint floods out until it meets the edges of the next enclosing area. Sometimes this means that you roll paint over the whole screen. If it is a garish colour you can always repeat the mistake with, say, white as the foreground colour.

7 Click the Text tool and click where you wish to begin typing. Your current foreground colour must be different from the background on which you propose to type.

8 Type **By Monet** in the drawing area. You can use the Backspace key to remove errors. Text is affected by various settings accessed through Font, Size and Style on the menu bar. Sizes followed by an asterisk in the Size menu give a better match between screen and printer fonts.

■ SECTION 17
Paintbrush

9 Type some more text in varying fonts, sizes and styles. Pressing the Enter key takes you on to the next line. If you click another part of the screen or choose a different tool, text is converted into graphics. As a result the normal Windows text editing conventions no longer apply to the text, you must edit the text as a graphic.

There are numerous ways of editing your work. You can try undo, Backspace, the erasers, the Scissors and the Pick tool.

10 Paint a line with the Brush tool and click Edit, Undo (or press Alt-Backspace). This removes all of the previous action. Edit, Undo a second time restores the action.

11 Paint another line and press the Backspace key. A square appears in the drawing area. The size of the square is determined by the current linesize. Drag the square cursor over the line. This removes part of the last action.

12 Click the Eraser tool and drag the eraser over your painting. The eraser changes the foreground colours into the current background colour. If the background colour is white then the foreground colours disappear. The width of the eraser is determined by the current linesize. Double clicking the Eraser clears everything and you are asked if you want to save your picture. Double clicking the Eraser is the same as File, New.

SECTION 17
Paintbrush

13 Click the Color Eraser tool and drag over your work. If you just tried double clicking the Eraser you should paint something first in various colours. The Color Eraser changes only the current foreground colour into the current background colour. Double clicking the Color Eraser changes every occurrence of the current foreground colour into the current background colour.

14 Click the Line tool and drag a few lines across the screen. Holding down the Shift key constrains the line to certain directions only. If you do not like the line, click the right hand mouse button before you stop dragging.

15 Click the Curve tool and drag the mouse to place a line in your painting.

16 Drag the mouse to one side of this line to produce a curve then click at the finish of the curve. You can draw an S-curve by not clicking at the finish, but dragging from the opposite side of the curve.

17 The bottom section of the Toolbox contains the Box, Rounded Box, Circle/Ellipse and the Polygon. These are shown in outline and the outline takes on the current foreground colour. To the right of each of these is the filled alternative. Filled shapes are filled in the current foreground colour and their outline is in the current background colour. Outline thicknesses depend upon the

SECTION 17
Paintbrush

current linesize. Holding down the Shift key constrains boxes as squares, and circles/ellipses as perfect circles.

Choose Box, Rounded Box, Circle/Ellipse in turn and drag the mouse after choosing each one to produce some interesting geometric designs.

18 Repeat step 17 with the filled alternatives, even if we are getting a little Euclidean!

19 Select either the Polygon or Filled Polygon tool. Drag the mouse to draw the first side of the polygon and let go of the mouse. Click in turn the remaining vertices of the polygon to draw additional sides. The last side is drawn automatically if you double click the position for the final vertex, or you could single click the first vertex.

The first two tools are the Scissors and the Pick tool. When chosen they let you select an area of the screen by dragging the mouse. Scissors is for selecting non-rectangular areas, Pick for rectangular areas. The selected area is called a cutout. Once you have defined a cutout you can cut it out, copy it and paste the copy somewhere else, all through the Edit menu. When a cutout is defined the Pick option on the menu bar is enabled. Through the Pick option you can flip the cutout horizontally and vertically, invert the colours, tilt it at an angle, enlarge it or shrink it. If you click Clear in the Pick menu the original is removed after any of these manipulations.

■ SECTION 17
Paintbrush

20 Click the Pick tool and drag over an area of your painting. Click Pick followed by Tilt. Position the cursor where you want a tilted copy and press and hold down the mouse button. Drag the mouse horizontally to produce a sheared rectangle and let go of the mouse button.

21 Practice flipping, shrinking and growing, and inverting a cutout.

22 While the cutout is still current, or define a new one, click Edit followed by Copy.

23 Alt-Tab back to Program Manager and start Cardfile.

24 In Cardfile choose File, Open and open the CUSTOMER file.

25 Bring the card for WEIRD NON-EUCLIDEAN THINGS to the front.

26 Click Edit in Cardfile followed by Picture.

SECTION 17
Paintbrush

27 Click Edit, Paste to place the cutout from Paintbrush on the card in Cardfile.

28 Drag the cutout into any position on the card then click Edit, Text. If the cutout is a large one you may lose some of the graphics off the edge of the card. A small cutout is better.

The index card now contains a company logo. This facility for pasting graphics onto cards is a convenient way to build up your own clipart library.

29 Close Cardfile and save your changes before Alt-Tabbing back to Paintbrush.

You will have noticed the scroll bars around the drawing area. Size of your painting can be larger than that shown on screen. You can move into the hidden areas with the scroll bars. The size

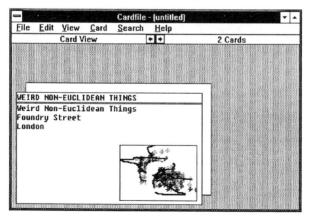

Graphic pasted into Cardfile

■ SECTION 17
Paintbrush

of the total drawing area is determined by Windows on the basis of your type of monitor, and memory available on your computer. You may override the defaults through Options, Image Attributes. The Image Attributes dialogue also enables you to work in black and white, if you have a colour monitor.

There are a number of methods of altering the amount of your picture showing on screen.

30 Click View, View Picture, or double click the Pick tool. This displays as much of the total picture area as possible on your monitor, though you can not edit in this mode. Click the picture once, or press Esc, to return to the default mode.

31 Click View then Zoom Out to see all of the picture area on screen. Your picture is scaled down to fit it in. The only editing options available in this mode work with cutouts. Click View, Zoom In to return to the default mode.

You can hide the Tools and Linesize, and the Palette sections through View to give you more room. This means you have to re-display them if you want to change tool, linesize or colour.

32 Click View then Zoom In. Place the resulting box over a part of your picture and click.

You will see a magnified image of the selected area where you may work on a pixel-by-pixel basis. This is valuable if you need to carry out detailed work. Clicking the left mouse

SECTION 17
Paintbrush

button on a pixel paints in the current foreground colour, the right button the background colour.

3 Alter a few pixels and click View, Zoom Out to judge the results. You will notice that the scaling produced by Zoom Out and Zoom In differs depending on which mode you are in.

To print your picture you would choose File, Print. The Print dialogue has various options. You are able to specify a draft-quality or proof-quality printout, to set the number of copies, to scale the picture, to print the whole picture or part of it, and to adapt printer resolution. The latter may result in a better definition of printout but is probably distorted.

Clicking File, Page Setup before File, Print allows you to format the printout. You can set margins and include headers and footers on the page. Headers and footers may contain date, time, page number, and filename as well as aligned text. There is a reference to formatting headers and footers in the Paintbrush chapter of the Windows User's Guide.

4 Click File, Save and enter the name **WEIRD** before clicking OK.

5 Close Paintbrush.

■ SECTION 18
Write

If you worked through Part Two you will have already used some of the features available in Write. This section is designed to give guidance on most of the remaining features.

1 Open and maximise Write.

2 Click File then Open.

3 Double click JANE.WRI. You may have to change directory to see JANE.WRI in the list box.

4 Select the whole document by holding down the Ctrl key while you click in the selection area to the left of the text.

The mouse pointer changes to an arrow when you are in the selection area. You may like to refer back to essential skills for information on selecting text. The keyboard equivalent for selecting all the text in a document is to press Ctrl-Home to take the cursor to the start of the document then, while holding down the Shift key press Ctrl-End to go to the end of the document.

All formatting options are available through the menu bar, whether accessed with a mouse or from the keyboard. A more convenient alternative for many of the options is to use the Ruler, although this requires a mouse.

■ SECTION 18
Write

5 Turn on the Ruler, if you have a mouse, by clicking Document followed by Ruler On.

6 Change the line spacing of your text to one and a half, then to two and back to single spacing. On the ruler this is carried out by clicking the appropriate line spacing icon. Otherwise you will have to click Paragraph and click 1½ Space (and Double Space and Single Space).

Many of the formatting options, like line spacing, can be set before typing or retrospectively, after typing. If they are set retrospectively, as we have just done, they apply to the selected text only. Remember you can select one word, one line, one sentence, a paragraph, or the whole text. You can also drag the mouse to select any area of text.

7 Change the justification of the whole text to centered, right aligned, fully justified and back to left aligned. On the ruler this is accomplished by clicking the relevant icon. From the menu bar click Paragraph then Centered (and Right, Justified and Left).

The Paragraph, Normal option always returns the selected text to left alignment with single line spacing.

You will notice that the previously centered letter head is now left aligned. This is because all the text was selected during the last step.

■ SECTION 18
Write

8 Drag the mouse over the letter head and centre it.

9 Now select the paragraph beginning *Thanks for your call.*

We will practice indenting this paragraph from the left and right margins. To do so you can use the Ruler, if you have a mouse, or Paragraph, Indents.

10 Indent the paragraph one inch from the left and right margins. From the Ruler you drag the left and right indent markers - the small black arrow heads. To drag the left-hand one you must first drag the small dot out the way. This dot is the first line indent marker. Position the left and right markers one inch further in from their original positions. Then go back to the small dot and drag it half an inch to the left of the left indent marker. This creates a paragraph of hanging indented text, after a first line of full width.

If you habitually use indentation then you could set the Ruler markers before you begin to type, rather than working retrospectively as here. Should you not have a mouse choose Paragraph then Indents. In the Indents dialogue set Left and Right Indent at one inch and First Line at minus half an inch (–0.5), before pressing the Enter key.

Default margins in Write are one inch for top and bottom, and 1.25 inches for left and right. These again may be altered before you start typing or adjusted afterwards. They can also be given different settings on different pages. You might wish to exper-

SECTION 18
Write

iment. If you set the left and right margins too narrow and/or your printer is set up for wide paper the text may scroll off the right hand edge of the screen. To see the hidden text use the horizontal scroll bar. Access to margin settings is through Document, Page Layout.

1 Select an individual word in the text, any word will do. This word is used to practise character formatting. With the word selected click Character and try choosing Bold, Italic, Underline, Superscript and Subscript in turn. You might like to choose two at the same time to see the effect. You might find it useful to click away from the word to remove the highlight in order to see the effects of format changes fully. Do not forget to reselect the text before changing format again. It is obviously not possible to have superscript and subscript at the same time. The Normal option removes any format changes from the word.

2 With the word selected, click Character once more and try all three fonts available in the Character menu. Some, or all, of these three can be used in conjunction with the Reduce Font and Enlarge Font options. The final entry in the Character menu, Fonts, gives access to all your fonts, should the three in the Character menu not be sufficient or appropriate.

While trying out some of these options take a look at Edit, Undo (Formatting) and see its effect on the selected word.

As you type Write inserts page breaks according to your paper size, and automatically suppresses widows and orphans. Widows

■ SECTION 18
Write

and orphans are single lines of text at the bottom or top of a page. To see page breaks choose File, Repaginate. To insert forced page breaks press Ctrl-Enter. In a long document you can jump directly to a specified page with Search, Go To Page.

The Search menu also includes Find, Repeat Last Find and Change. Find jumps straight to the first occurrence, after the cursor position, of a specified entry. Change goes to the defined text and replaces it with any alternative text you enter in the Change dialogue. Repeat Last Find repeats the last Find or Change carried out.

Write offers the facility to include headers and footers in your document. Both headers and footers can be configured to automatically paginate your text. They are defined through Document, Header or Document, Footer.

Write has default tabs, that is left tabs, set at every half an inch. If you wish you can create your owns, whether left or decimal tabs. Any user-defined setting overrides the default settings, which are not shown anywhere. With the Ruler you click the icon for left or decimal tabs and then click at the required position immediately below the Ruler. Once in place tab markers are easily dragged from side to side. To remove a tab drag it off the bottom of the Ruler. Without the Ruler it is necessary to go through Document, Tabs. In the subsequent Tabs dialogue the position of each tab has to be typed in. The Decimal check box is for defining a decimal rather than a left tab. Note that the Write default tab positions do not appear in this dialogue. Any entries you make take precedence over the hidden default settings. Individual tabs are adjusted by editing their entry in the Positions box. All the user-defined tabs can be removed by clicking Clear All.

SECTION 18
Write

13 Experiment as much as you like with JANE.WRI, as we will not be needing it any more. Try and incorporate some features covered in previous steps and text. When you are reasonably happy that you understand how to access the facilities in Write, print the document to see the results of your editing. To print, click File, Print, OK.

The Print dialogue that appears, before you click OK, contains a couple of parameters. You are able to print one or more copies, print all or a range of pages, and print in draft-quality. Draft-quality is ideal if you are in a hurry, though the text is unformatted and any graphics print as empty boxes only.

PART FIVE

Windows Applications

■ SECTION 19
Word Processors

This section and the remaining sections in Part Five are for those who wish to move forward and really exploit all the benefits promised by Windows 3. Windows alone is fine and more than adequate for the requirements of many people. If you have gone through all exercises in the book, you will have had a taste of what Windows by itself has to offer. If you are completely satisfied with what you have seen then perhaps you will not have to consider the purchase of additional applications. Though for a lot of readers the facilities offered by the accessories like Write, Paintbrush, and Cardfile are not really suited to serious home or business use. I have in mind features like mail merge, spell checking, Bezier curves, relating database files together, and desktop publishing.

Buying Windows-based applications confers numerous advantages. First, they all have a similar look and feel, so learning times should be drastically reduced and productivity increased when compared with standard non-Windows applications. Second, they provide a range of features that surpasses those available with the bundled Windows accessories. Third, memory permitting, you can multi-task two or more of these applications, there is no more sitting around waiting for a process to finish in one. Fourth, they support clipboarding, so text and graphics data is easily swapped from application to application. Fifth, many of them support DDE (dynamic data exchange), which may be used to protect the accuracy of data held in the files for more than one application. Sixth, some of them work with DLLs (dynamic link libraries), enabling parameters to be passed to, and received from, non-Windows applications. Seventh, the fact that they operate under Windows means applications are no longer subject to the DOS memory limit. Eighth, Windows versions of some applications are the same as OS/2 versions. If you were ever to switch from DOS to OS/2 then little retraining is involved.

SECTION 19
Word Processors

In the discussions that follow applications have been categorised by type, for instance, word processors and desktop publishing. There is however a lot of overlap between some of the categories and the traditional sharp divisions between types of applications are becoming increasingly blurred. Not only are these categorisations a little arbitrary but so to is my choice of packages. When it was first launched in 1990 there were already quite a few applications ready to work with Windows 3. In the space of only six months, from launch to time of writing, literally hundreds of Windows 3-compatible products have come to market. This trend looks set to continue. Hopefully the packages I have chosen are among the better ones, althoguh it is impossible to evaluate hundreds of applications and there are probably some highly deserving applications I have not managed to see, let alone recommend. The criteria used in choosing applications are based on the popularity and wide availability of software, consensus opinion among reviewers, my own feelings about packages, and my own testing of all the packages referred too. Needless to say I have been heavily influenced by those applications I use on a regular basis, for they have become personal favourites and are tried and tested as a suite of programs.

Please note that you will need plenty of room on your hard disk to accommodate applications, typically one to three megabytes per application. Some of the more powerful applications require at least an 80286 processor and plenty of memeory. Please contact your software dealer for full details.

Also ensure you buy a version of the application fully compatible with Windows 3. Some Windows-based applications are written for Windows 2 and as such, earlier versions do not work with Windows 3 in standard or enhanced mode.

SECTION 19
Word Processors

Write

Write is, of course, bundled with Windows, and is mentioned by way of comparison only. The Write accessory is a word processor and includes some quite handy features. We have already met some of its capabilities – changing fonts, centring text, pasting in graphics and text, and basic character formats. There are other features too, mentioned almost in passing – a Go To page option, search and replace, forced page breaks, indentation and two types of tabs, justification, line spacing, headers and footers, page numbering, draft and final copy printing, and margin settings.

If the features listed for Write are sufficient then there is no need to find another couple of hundred pounds for a heavy-weight word processor. If, however, you want to run a mail merge, carry out a spell check, use pre-defined styles and templates, control hyphenation of justified text, automate tasks with a macro, view your whole page before printing, generate an index or table of contents, insert footnotes, include equations and symbols, create tables, sort data, or do a word count, then you will have to look further afield. The best known and most popular word processors for Windows are Ami, Ami Professional and Word for Windows. There is also a promising newcomer called Legacy, and not long after this book reaches the bookshops you might be considering something called WordPerfect for Windows. WordPerfect is one of the best non-Windows word processors and was my workhorse before I switched over to Windows. A version of WordPerfect for Windows sounds quite interesting and will certainly be worth a look. In the meantime the real choice seems to be between the two Ami word processors and Word for Windows.

■ SECTION 19
Word Processors

Ami

Ami is frequently referred to as a middle-weight word processor. Given its range of features it lies somewhere halfway between Write and its stable-mate Ami Professional. It is also cheaper than Ami Professional and the other heavy-weight, Word for Windows. Some reviewers have described it as an entry-level word processor. It possesses all of the capability of Write and more. There are two extra types of tabs, a greater choice of character formats, a spell checker, mail merge, the ability to crop and rotate graphics, hyphenation, support for styles and multi-column pages. You can view your document full-page, use macros, and export and import data in a variety of formats. It works with DDE which Write does not.

Ami Professional

One of the two early contenders in the battle to emerge as the de facto standard word processor for Windows, the other being Word for Windows. Ami Professional is a fine piece of software and has received a fair amount of publicity. It has all that Ami has, but a lot more besides. You can customise menus, draw charts and graphics, generate an index and table of contents, include tables, perform calculations, sort data, use a thesaurus, and process TIFF files.

The consensus seems to be that Ami Professional is to be preferred to Word for Windows in areas like handling graphics and drawing lines on pages. Ami Professional includes a graphics toolbox which Word for Windows does not.

SECTION 19
Word Processors

Word for Windows

Word for Windows is directly comparable with Ami Professional. It lacks some of the graphics capabilities of Ami Professional, otherwise the two applications are more or less similar in their range of features. Many reviews have involved a head-on clash between the two, and Ami Professional tends to lose out on speed, though I have seen figures appearing to contradict this finding. In reality there is little to choose between the two and purely subjective judgements may well sway the balance. Word for Windows gives the impression of being a more solid piece of work, even if there are strange omissions. Word for Windows happens to be my choice at the moment and I use it as my day-to-day word processor. This book was written entirely in Word for Windows, and despite a few glitches, it handles a file of forty thousand words with consummate ease. I recommend its outlining capabilities.

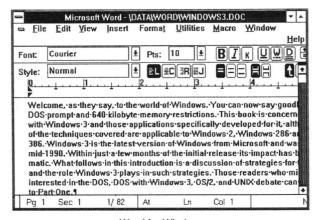

Word for Windows

SECTION 20
Desktop Publishing

As Ami, Ami Professional and Word for Windows can cope with graphics and allow you to work in full-page view, they are in fact doing the work of a desktop publishing package. Having said that, there is nothing quite as good as a dedicated desktop publishing application. Because they are designed specifically for the task they are so much better at it than heavy-weight word processors. If your business involves publishing, page layout, a lot of cutting and pasting from and on to pages, extensive use of graphics, then you might find a Windows word processor is not up to the job.

PageMaker and Ventura

PageMaker has been around for some time and is well tried and tested. Ventura for Windows is a relatively new and not so well proven, though the GEM version of Ventura is much admired in the professional DTP world. Ventura and PageMaker both have their devotees and it has to be admitted both have their strong points. In reality I suppose it makes little difference which one you eventually plump for. I am personally undecided and will therefore try and give a consensus opinion. PageMaker (version 3.01 is fully Windows 3-compatible) is generally more fun and more comfortable to use. It is ideal for short publications – brochures, posters, articles and so on – though it will cope with documents of well over one hundred pages. Ventura is often the selection of the serious publisher and is generally considered to be just that little bit more powerful and to include rather more in the way of features. For example it handles tables and index generation as well as interactively updating imported text. Ventura is usually preferred for longer documents. I use both and tend to follow the classic divide of PageMaker for short pieces and Ventura for longer stuff. The eventual release of PageMaker 4 will probably make a complete nonsense of this divide. This book is laid out and prepared for printing in Ventura.

SECTION 20
Desktop Publishing

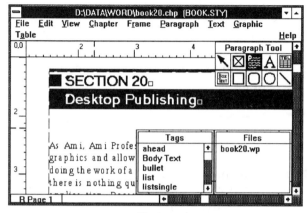

Ventura

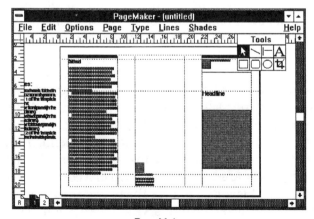

PageMaker

■ SECTION 21
Spreadsheets

For a long time the sole representative of a spreadsheet for Windows was Excel. This has been quietly chipping away at the established base of standard spreadsheets like Lotus 1-2-3 and Supercalc. There is now some Windows competition for Excel in the form of Wingz. And soon Lotus will be replying with a version of 1-2-3 for Windows.

Excel

Excel (version 2.1c is fully Windows 3 compatible) is a classic spreadsheet and is rapidly gaining in popularity. It looks and feels right, though some of its detractors find it a little slow and cumbersome. The charts that are produced to reflect figures in the spreadsheet are excellent, though unfortunately there is no 3D option. Excel version 3 is a major revision and incorporates many of the features detailed below for Wingz, including 3D charting.

Wingz

Wingz is one of many applications that started life on the Apple Macintosh and eventually migrated to Windows on the PC. At the time of writing it represents the only real challenge to Excel as the spreadsheet to use with Windows.

Wingz is rather more than a simple spreadsheet, and those accustomed to Lotus 1-2-3 or Supercalc might be slightly overwhelmed by its range of features. The minimum amount of RAM you needed is two megabytes, while the recommended memory is a massive three megabytes. I say massive guardedly, for four or more megabytes of RAM will be the norm in a couple of years. The spreadsheet itself is a grid of over thirty two thousand rows and over thirty two thousand columns. Graphics capabilities are more advanced than Excel's, and include the ability to draw and rotate

■ SECTION 21
Spreadsheets

Excel

3D charts. A toolbox provides freehand drawing facilities and you can import bit-mapped and scanned images. In addition blocks of text can be imported or pasted in from other applications. The permutations of features in Wingz are virtually endless and it looks set to do for spreadsheets what Superbase 4 is already doing for databases. For example you can show cells, charts, text boxes, explanatory graphics and customised pushbuttons on screen at the same time.

SECTION 22
Databases

There are already quite a number of databases around for Windows 3. The standard non-Windows database is of course dBase but Ashton-Tate, the supplier of dBase, has not announced any intentions of writing a Windows version of dBase. However there are Windows front ends for dBase, like dBFast/Windows from Bumble Bee Software.

The main contenders for the status of being the standard database for Windows appear to be Superbase 2, Superbase 4 and Omnis 5, with the majority opting for Superbase 4.

Superbase 2

This is perhaps one of the most intuitive databases on the market. The most noticeable feature is perhaps the video recorder controls at the bottom of the screen, enabling the user to browse easily through the records in the database. Facilities exist to incorporate external text files as fields and even graphics. A personnel file, for example, might contain a scanned photograph for each employee record. Data validation and record filters are simply constructed by clicking fieldnames and operators – no need to type lengthy commands from the keyboard. Macros can be used to record and automate repetitive tasks. A database file can be customised for data entry, or editing, or browsing with forms. The forms are created in the Form Painter which has its own toolbox for special graphics effects. Forms are an excellent way in which to view and edit more than one database file at once. Superbase 2 (release 1.2 is fully Windows 3-compatible) also acts as a run-time version of Superbase so that programmed applications developed in Superbase 4 can be run.

SECTION 22
Databases

Superbase 4

The big brother of Superbase 2, Superbase 4 is a true heavyweight database. It abounds in features and is so versatile you have to see it in operation – a written description simply can not convey its real potential. Yet it is not difficult to learn. Superbase 4 (release 1.2 or higher is recommended for use with Windows 3) has all the capability of Superbase 2 and a whole lot more. Form Designer replaces the Form Painter available with Superbase 2 and extends its options. For example pushbuttons may be put on forms which call program sub-routines when activated. Form Designer also includes a powerful report generator. Superbase 4 incorporates a programming language called *database management language* (DML) which allows the construction of very sophisticated customised applications. There are a number of levels on which to use Superbase 4 and these levels can call each other if required – native mode, macros, forms and programs. Perhaps the only criticism of Superbase 4 is that, precisely because it offers so much, it is sometimes difficult to decide between alternatives. A successful application inspires third parties to create add-ons for the application and this is already beginning to happen with Superbase. Da Vinci produces Live Link which captures video images as graphics fields. Bits Per Second has recently launched Chartbuilder. Chartbuilder takes data from a Superbase file and creates charts on the basis of the data, the charts being in either 2D or 3D.

Omnis 5

Omnis 5 is another powerful application and provides a range of graphics and programmable features. If you want you can build an application making Omnis 5 almost transparent to the user and indeed bearing little relationship to the traditional concept of a database. Omnis 5 has the capability of acting as a front end to

SECTION 22
Databases

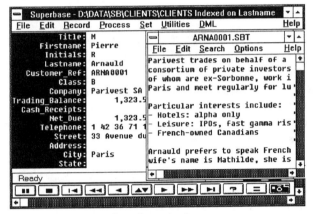

Superbase database

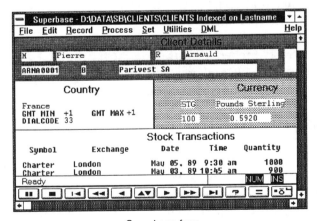

Superbase form

■ SECTION 22
Databases

SQL databases on a mini or mainframe computer. Another valuable asset is the ability to open multiple windows, with each window containing different but related information in the form of fields, text and graphics. Some software reviews are quite complementary to Omnis 5 though the consensus seems to be that Superbase is, if anything more powerful, and easier to get to grips with.

■ SECTION 23
Graphics

The large variety of applications encompassed by the term *graphics* has led to that term being divided into more exact categories. So you are likely to come across references to charting, painting, drawing and presentation graphics. All of these categories represent a difference of emphasis, though some applications straddle two or more of the categories.

Charting is the production of 2D or 3D charts (graphs) based upon a series of data values. Under Windows 3 this is traditionally done by exporting the data to Excel and instructing Excel to draw the chart. If DDE links have been defined then the chart is automatically updated to match changes in the original data. An alternative is to export figures to a presentation graphics program. Or you could use a dedicated charting application. As previously mentioned Bits Per Second has released Chartbuilder for Superbase and versions are in the pipeline for use with Excel and Word for Windows.

Painting refers to the creation of bit-mapped graphics. The Windows accessory Paintbrush is a painting package. Bit-mapped graphics are fine for simple applications especially if there are no curves. However, stretching or scaling of bit-mapped graphics, or the inclusion of curves, results in a bitty appearance, both on screen and on printout. This bitty appearance, where curves for instance have a ragged edge, is sometimes referred to as *jaggies*. Paintbrush itself is quite a good painting application and it is unlikely that the average user would wish to consider anything from third parties.

Drawing applications do not normally create bit-mapped graphics. As a result the graphics are more amenable to stretching or scaling and curves (Bezier curves) look more natural. Two front runners in the Windows drawing package race are Corel Draw and Micrografx Designer. Both these packages have received

SECTION 23
Graphics

enthusiastic reviews, though Corel appears the most popular and is my recommendation. An added bonus with Corel Draw and Designer is the inclusion of large libraries of pre-drawn graphics, or clip art.

Presentation graphics are graphics designed for showing to audiences at conferences, launches, sales meetings, seminars and so on. Highly customised charts are often produced as well as graphics suitable for overhead transparencies and slide shows. Both Micrografx Charisma and Powerpoint from Microsoft are well represented in this field.

A further category which may be included under the heading graphics is CAD (computer aided design). An example of software in this category is Drafix Windows CAD.

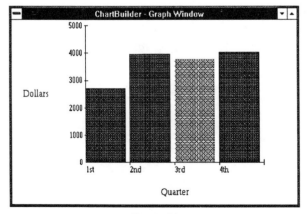

Chartbuilder

SECTION 23
Graphics

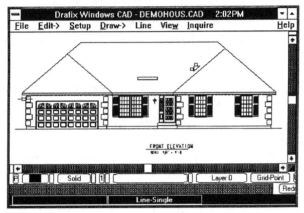

Windows CAD

■ SECTION 24
Time and project management

This category of software applications covers the area sometimes called office planning. Office planning embraces such concepts as recording appointments, scheduling meetings, keeping things-to-do lists, prioritising tasks, and viewing and co-ordinating the component parts of a larger project. The latter often involves manipulation of Gantt charts. Complex projects are sometimes handled with critical path analysis. Time and project management software facilitates some or all of these features of office planning, either on an individual employee or an office-wide basis. Applications worth considering include IBM Current, Microsoft Project and Planisoft from CPS.

SECTION 25
Development work

By development work I mean building your own Windows-based applications from scratch. This is not as difficult as it might sound. In packages like Superbase and Excel you can create customised database and spreadsheet applications. Even if the original application is made more-or-less transparent you are still working with database and spreadsheet files and are limited ultimately by the capabilities of the software, although the ability to access dynamic link libraries (DLLs) greatly extends functionality. If you require even more flexibility then a development program might be necessary. These allow the user to set up windows, menus, dialogue boxes, scroll bars, pushbuttons, check boxes, option buttons, list boxes, text boxes, text and hypertext, graphics and hypergraphics to suit. Although Superbase 4, for example, is capable of many of these, it is a database and does not offer the flexibility of a full development package. Incidentally, hypertext is an area of text, sensitive to a mouse click, leads to another display of text and/or graphics. Hypergraphics do the same with graphics on screen. Hypertext and hypergraphics are ideal for moving through large amounts of information, accurately and swiftly.

The software provided to developers by Microsoft, the supplier of Windows, is the SDK (Software Development Kit). This is probably best left to advanced users only; those wishing to write and market their own applications. The intermediate user might take a look at KnowledgePro or Toolbook. To those of you who might shudder (like myself) at the thought of heavy, technical, low-level programming the following Knowledge Pro routine might reassure you:

    window (,20,10,50,15, 'My Window').

    text ('

SECTION 25
Development work

This is my very

own window

').

button (Quit).

This routine displays a window complete with scroll bars, title bar, borders and a Control menu. Numbers represent column and row positions of the top left-hand corner of the window, together with window width and height. The entry in the title bar reads *My Window*, while contents of the window is the text *This is my very own window* with a pushbutton saying *Quit*.

There is a packet bundled with Windows 3, containing a run-time version of Toolbook. The instructions for installing this run-time version are on the outside of the packet. Being a run-time version it does not let you write actual applications, but runs applications developed with the full version of Toolbook. One example application that is included is called Daybook and gives an idea of what can be accomplished with a full version of Toolbook.

SECTION 26
Fontware

This is not the place to enter into a technical discussion of the different styles of fonts. Suffice it to say that the font actually printed by your printer is often different from the font shown on screen. This is particularly noticeable when word processing. Windows word processors use a graphics screen. This allows you to see a fair representation of the typeface, size and style of your text on screen. When the screen display matches the printout it is called a WYSIWYG display. WYSIWYG is an acronym for *what you see is what you get*. Many Windows applications give you a more-or-less WYSIWYG display. However if the font used by Windows to put the text on screen does not exactly correspond to the font used by your printer, it is not full WYSIWYG. For example, in Word for Windows, you may see a line of text extending beyond the right-hand margin of the page in Page View. Windows has attempted to find a screen font that matches, as closely as possible, size, typeface and style of the font selected for printing. In this example the nearest screen font available is wider than the printer font and hence the same line of text takes up more room on screen, and goes past the right hand-margin. When you print, however, the same line of text stops at the margin.

It is more important to see line breaks, the word on which the line ends, than to have a neat display with all the text wrapping at or before the margin. If you are lucky, on the other hand, your printer might have the same fonts as the Windows screen fonts, in which case you have the best of both worlds – you see the correct point of the line break while the screen wraps the text at or before the right margin. Try varying the font in a trial document and see if you can achieve a true WYSIWYG display for one or more fonts. Should this not be possible and you want this full WYSIWYG display, you will have to install extra screen fonts that are replicas of your chosen printer fonts. There are a couple of packages around that allow you to do just this, whether for a dot matrix, HP Laserjet-compatible or Postscript-compatible laser printer. In

SECTION 26
Fontware

addition they improve the sometimes bitty appearance of characters on the screen. Bitstream markets FaceLift which includes thirteen matching screen and printer fonts from the standard Swiss (Helvetica) and Dutch (Times Roman) fonts to more exotic fonts like Park Avenue and Formal Script (Ondine). You can buy extension packs which greatly increase the number of true WYSIWYG fonts available. Another alternative is Type Manager from Adobe which is very similar to FaceLift. A later version of Windows could well include true WYSIWYG screen and printer fonts as standard.

SECTION 27
UNIX links

The two main trends in business computing involve different operating systems. First there is a large established base of UNIX (and Xenix) computers and applications. This section is growing despite the fact that UNIX is quite an old operating system. Second there are millions of PCs running DOS, and within this section more and more users are turning to Windows 3. One recent estimate suggests that half of all PCs will have Windows 3 installed within the next two years. OS/2 is a newer operating system which has yet to make its true impact. The situation in many businesses is one where an established multi-user system, based on UNIX, coexists with a PC-based system running Windows 3 under DOS. Windows makes it possible to link systems together and to run UNIX applications under Windows on a PC. The join between the two systems can be made seamless and transparent to the PC user. For example they might wish to access the UNIX text editor VI, and as far as they are concerned it is only another application in a window.

JSB have a package called Multiview Desktop which sets up the link between Windows and UNIX. It adds an icon for UNIX to a Program Manager group. Double clicking the UNIX icon provides a gateway into a remote UNIX machine, and applications on that machine can be started on the PC. VI, for example, could be run in a window concurrently with Windows accessories and applications. The UNIX application may be minimised or maximised just as any other window. Data may be cut, copied and pasted between UNIX and Windows applications and data from the remote UNIX application can be printed locally from Windows.

A recent announcement from JSB takes this a step further with a new product called Multiview Deskterm. Deskterm actually turns the UNIX application into something approaching a true Windows-based application, with some of the Windows generic menu bar options. Those readers who have some experience of

SECTION 27
UNIX links

arcane UNIX applications will appreciate being able to click File, Open and File, Save.

There is now a wide variety of products that forge the Windows-to-UNIX link: PC Connect and SQL Connect are just two. With these products, for instance, it is possible to read data from an SQL database on a remote UNIX machine into Superbase on a local PC.

SECTION 28
Utilities

The Windows add-on market is growing rapidly, with a plethora of handy utilities. If Windows itself, Windows accessories and Windows-based applications do not meet all of your needs then there is a utility somewhere to plug the gap.

One of the better known suppliers of Windows utilities is HDC. HDC markets a number of utilities with names like MicroApps, FirstApps, and Windows Express. Some of these utilities are especially valuable. I had in mind one that recovers accidentally deleted files and another that saves the screen. A screen saver blanks the screen after a defined period of mouse and keyboard inactivity. This prevents phosphor burn-in which leaves an ugly ghost image on the monitor. Clicking the mouse, or pressing a key, restores the screen. Other utilities from HDC let you design your own icons, view the physical location of files on a disk, see which programs are using up memory, put password protection on selected icons, and automatically save data at regular intervals. And if you get tired you can always have a cuddly, animated dinosaur stroll across the screen or play Rocks.

There are literally hundreds of Windows applications and utilities currently available. Many are reviewed in the major computer magazines and some distributors specialise in Windows software. The Windows Shopper's Guide, published in the USA, is a good source of information about Windows products. As I write a couple of magazines, dedicated to Windows, are about to be launched in the UK. In the UK too NEOW, Frontline, and Xitan stock most of the popular Windows applications and utilities.

SECTION 28
Utilities

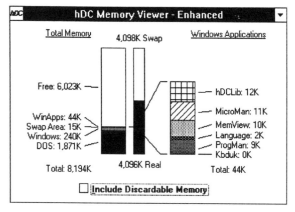

FirstApps

APPENDICES

APPENDIX A
Further accessories

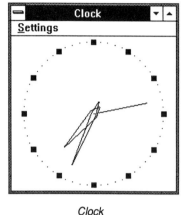

Clock

Clock

When you start Clock the Settings menu allows you to switch between a digital and an analogue clock. A minimised Clock can keep ticking away at the bottom of the screen, should you need to see the time.

PIF Editor

It is extremely unlikely that you will ever need to use PIF Editor. It is there to provide consistency with earlier versions of Windows, users of Windows 2 may have PIF files they might want to adapt for use with Windows 3. It is also available to fine tune the way in which a non-Windows application runs under Windows. This could be necessary if the application fails to work or it behaves unpredictably. I would strongly recommend you use Windows applications rather than standard applications. Windows applications do not have PIF files. If you do run your old favourite standard applications from Windows then they will work fine

APPENDIX A
Further accessories

PIF Editor

without a PIF. In the rare event this is not true and you are determined to carry on, then you are referred to Chapter 12 More About Applications in the Windows User's Guide.

Terminal

It is impossible to provide a step-by-step guide to Terminal, even for those of you who have a modem. The reason is quite simply that Terminal involves the setting of literally dozens of parameters, any or all of which differ from reader to reader. The basic procedures in operating Terminal are opening Terminal, entering a phone number, setting your computer's terminal emulation, setting your terminal parameters, choosing communications and modem settings, and then sending or receiving text or binary files. The interested reader is referred to Chapter 9 in the Windows User's Guide. You should be aware of the type and capabilities of your modem, the terminal emulation required by the remote computer, and protocols involved in talking to that computer.

APPENDIX A
Further accessories

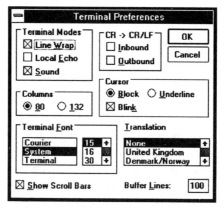

A typical Terminal dialogue

■ APPENDIX B
Networks

Windows 3 is compatible with most popular network software. There are two options for having Windows on a network. The first is to have one copy of Windows on the file server, shared by all the network users. The second is for each user to have a completely separate copy of Windows on a local hard disk.

If you adopt the latter approach then there is usually little extra configuration necessary – network software itself handles all network operations, provided you install the network software correctly in the first place. For example, to print on a remote printer simply click File, Print as normal. To copy files between the file server and your local hard disk open File Manager, which displays one or more extra icons for the file server hard disk. To run a multi-user version of a separate Windows application double click its icon in Program Manager – though you will have to consult the application manual to set up the icon correctly.

If you are sharing one copy of Windows across a network you might like to customise Windows for your own workstation. Some files will be available to you only, and can reside on your local hard disk or in your user directory on the file server, although you will still be sharing most of the Windows files with others. To customise Windows for your own workstation type SETUP/N at your local DOS prompt, after the shared copy has been installed by the network administrator.

Given the complexity of network software you will probably experience a few teething problems. These can usually be sorted out by first checking the network software installation and then some of the Windows defaults. These defaults are shown in the SYSTEM.INI and WIN.INI files. Some defaults are covered in Chapter 14 of the Windows User's Guide. Further information, in great detail, is contained in the NETWORKS.TXT file. This is a text file and may be read in and printed out from Notepad.

APPENDIX C
Swapfiles

When Windows runs in enhanced mode, that is on a 386/486 computer with a minimum of two megabytes of RAM, it is able to exploit virtual memory. Virtual memory is a pseudo-memory created on the hard disk. Windows swaps itself from real memory (RAM) to virtual memory when real memory begins to run low. In effect, virtual memory increases the amount of memory in your computer. And more memory increases speed of execution of applications and allows more applications to be open simultaneously. Windows sets up virtual memory by automatically creating a temporary swap file on the hard disk. Efficiency of such a swap file is greatly increased by designating part of the hard disk as a permanent swap file. Such a permanent swap file is not available for any other use and you should only set one up if you have plenty of room on your hard disk. Space occupied by a permanent swap file must be in a contiguous area of the hard disk. To increase the size of a free contiguous area on a hard disk you might find it advisable to run a special utility first, Norton's Speed Disk for instance.

Procedure for setting up a permanent swap file is quite straightforward (your computer must be capable of running Windows in enhanced mode) :

1 Exit from Windows.

2 Force Windows to start in real mode by entering **WIN/R** at the DOS prompt.

■ APPENDIX C
Swapfiles

3 Close any applications that you might have configured to load with Windows – only Program Manager should be open.

4 Click File then Run, type **SWAPFILE** in the dialogue, and click OK

The subsequent dialogue is the Swapfile dialogue. In this dialogue Windows recommends the best size for your swap file, based on its scrutiny of your hard disk. You would normally want to accept this default though you may change it if you wish.

5 Click Create to accept the permanent swap file size. Or click Cancel to back out of the whole procedure.

6 Exit Windows and restart Windows in enhanced mode by typing **WIN**.

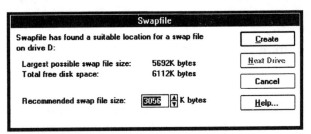

Swapfile dialogue

APPENDIX C
Swapfiles

You can change the swap file at any time, or delete it, by repeating steps 1 to 4. An existing permanent swap file results in a different Swapfile dialogue which has options to either delete, or delete and create a new (that is change) swap file .

INDEX

Index

386 Enhanced Icon, 161
386 mode
   See Enhanced mode

A

Accessories group, 42, 55, 95
Activating a printer, 30
Alt-Enter, 164
Alt-Esc, 60, 62
Alt-Print Screen, 163
Alt-Tab, 59, 60, 62, 63
Ami, 199, 200
Ami Professional, 95, 199, 200
Apple Macintosh, 12, 204
Application icons, 43
Application windows, 43
Applications setting, 30
Associations, 134
AUTOEXEC.BAT, 33
AUTOEXEC.BAT, modifying, 26

B

Bezier curves, 210
BMP format, 103, 178
Border, 43
BUFFERS, 33

C

CAD, 211
Calculator, 96, 120
   Edit, Copy, 121
Calendar, 96, 105
   File, Save, 107
Camera ready copy, 7
Cancelling, 49
Cardfile, 96, 107, 170
   bringing to front, 173
   Card, Add, 108, 171
   Card, Autodial, 176
   Card, Delete, 175
   Card, Duplicate, 175
   Edit, Copy, 124, 175
   Edit, Cut, 175
   Edit, Index, 174
   Edit, Paste, 175, 185
   Edit, Picture, 177, 184
   Edit, Restore, 176
   Edit, Text, 177, 185
   Edit, Undo, 176
   File Print, 175
   File, Merge, 177
   File, Open, 124
   File, Print All, 175
   File, Save, 109, 177
   File, Save As, 177
   Search, Find, 109, 174
   Search, Find Next, 174
   Search, Go To, 109, 173
   sorting cards, 172
   View, List, 109, 174
Cascading, 64
Cascading menus, 75
Changing directories, 78
Charisma, 211
Chartbuilder, 207, 210
Charting, 210
Check boxes, 80
Chevron, double, 79
Clicking, 45
Clipboard, 7, 41, 119, 121, 163
   Edit, Delete, 163
   File, Open, 163
   File, Save, 163
Clock, 96, 225
CLP format, 163
Cold links, 123
Color Icon, 88, 151
Colour schemes, 90
Command buttons, 79
Computer aided design, 211
Computer setting, 22
CONFIG.SYS, 33
CONFIG.SYS, modifying, 26
Configuration, 19
Control menu, 37, 43

Index

Control Panel, 88, 151
Copy, 85
Copying application icons, 146
Copying files, 138
Corel Draw, 96, 210
Corner, 43
CRC, 7
Creating a swapfile, 230
Creating application icons, 144
Creating groups, 143
CrossTalk, 96
Ctrl-Break, 112
Ctrl-Esc, 60, 62
Ctrl-Tab, 73
Currency format, 157
Current, 96, 213
Cursor, blink rate, 160
Cut, 85
Cycling application windows, 62
Cycling document windows, 73
Cycling in a dialogue box, 77

D

Database management language, 207
Databases, 206
Date format, 157
Date/Time Icon, 159
Daybook, 215
dBase, 11, 206
dBFast/Windows, 206
DDE, 14, 123, 197, 210
Default directory, 21
Default mode, 35
Deleting application icons, 145
Deleting files, 139
Deleting groups, 144
Designer, 96, 210
Desktop Icon, 159
Desktop publishing, 202
Desqview, 11
Dialogue boxes, 49, 76
Dialogue boxes, cancelling, 49
Dimmed entries, 74

DLL, 197, 214
DML, 207
Document icons
  See Group icons
Document windows, 43
DOS, 11
DOS Icon, 164
DOS in a window, 164
Double click speed, 158
Double clicking, 45
Dragging, 45
Drawing, 210
DRDOS, 11
Drop-down list boxes, 88
Dynacomm, 96
Dynamic data exchange, 14, 123, 197, 210
Dynamic link libraries, 197

E

Edit, Copy, 85
Edit, Cut, 85
Edit, Paste, 85
EGA.SYS, 34
Ellipsis, 74, 79
Enhanced mode, 34, 229
Esc, 79
Excel, 64, 95, 96, 123, 204, 210, 214
Exiting Windows, 37

F

FaceLift, 217
File Manager, 131
  changing drives, 132
  copying a disk, 133
  Disk, 133
  displaying files, 136
  File, Associate, 134
  File, Copy, 133, 138
  File, Create Directory, 133
  File, Delete, 133, 139

Index

File, Move, 133, 138
File, Open, 133
File, Rename, 133
File, Search, 133
  formatting a disk, 133
  labelling a disk, 133
  Options, Confirmation, 132, 137
  Tree, Collapse Branch, 134
  Tree, Expand One Level, 135
  warning, 131
File menu, 37
File, Print, 36
FILES, 33
FirstApps, 220
Fonts
  adding, 156
  removing, 156
Fonts Icon, 156
Fontware, 216

G

Games group, 42, 52
GEM, 13, 202
Graphical user interface, 13
Graphics, 210
Grayed entries, 74
Group icons, 44, 55
GUI, 13

H

Hardware settings, 22
Help, 85
Help, Index, 85
HIMEM.SYS, 33
Hot links, 123
Hypergraphics, 214
Hypertext, 214

I

Icons, 43
Initial screen, 32, 41

Installation, 19
International Icon, 157

J

Jaggies, 210

K

Keyboard Icon, 158
Keyboard Layout setting, 24
Keyboard setting, 23
KnowledgePro, 214

L

Language, 157
Language setting, 24
Legacy, 199
List boxes, 76
Live Link, 207
Lotus 1-2-3, 11, 204

M

Macros, 109, 113
Main group, 41, 95
Maximise button, 43
Maximising a window, 49
Menu bar, 43
Menus, 74
MicroApps, 220
Minimise button, 43
Minimising a window, 50
Mouse
  actions, 44
  clicking, 45
  compatible, 40
  double clicking, 45
  dragging, 45
  Icon, 158
  moving, 45
  right clicking, 46
  setting, 23

237

Index

tracking speed, 159
Moving a window, 67
Moving application icons, 146
Moving files, 138
MSDOS, 11
MSP format, 178
Multi-tasking, 64
Multiview Deskterm, 218
Multiview Desktop, 218

N

Network Icon, 161
Network setting, 24
Networks, 228
NETWORKS.TXT, 228
Non-Windows Applications group, 42, 55, 95
Notepad, 57, 97, 104
    Edit, 74
    Edit, Copy, 112, 122
    Edit, Word Wrap, 104
    File, 74
    File, Open, 75, 122
    File, Save, 105
    Search, Find, 80

O

Omnis 5, 96, 207
Open Desktop, 13
Open Look, 13
Opening screen, 32, 41
Option buttons, 81
OS/2, 11, 12, 197, 218

P

PageMaker, 7, 98, 202
Paintbrush, 7, 56, 95, 99, 178, 210
    Airbrush tool, 179
    background colour, 100
    Box tool, 182
    Brush tool, 179, 181
    Circle/Ellipse tool, 182
    Color Eraser tool, 182
    Curve tool, 182
    Edit, Copy, 125, 184
    Edit, Undo, 181
    Eraser tool, 102, 181
    File, New, 101, 181
    File, Open, 125
    File, Page Setup, 187
    File, Print, 103, 187
    File, Save, 102, 187
    File, Save As, 102
    Filled Box tool, 100, 101
    Filled Circle tool, 101
    Filled Polygon tool, 183
    Font, 180
    foreground colour, 100
    Line tool, 182
    Linesize, 99, 179
    Options, 179
    Options, Image Attributes, 186
    Paint Roller tool, 180
    Palette, 99
    Pick, 183
    Pick tool, 125, 181, 183
    Pick, Clear, 183
    Pick, Tilt, 184
    Polygon tool, 182
    Roller tool, 180
    Rounded Box tool, 182
    Scissors tool, 181, 183
    Size, 180
    Style, 180
    Text tool, 180
    Toolbox, 99, 100
    View, Palette, 100
    View, Tools & Linesize, 100
    View, View Picture, 186
    View, Zoom In, 100, 186
    View, Zoom Out, 100, 186
Painting, 210
Paper size setting, 29
Parent directory, 79
Paste, 85

Index

PC Connect, 219
PCDOS, 11
PCX format, 103, 178
PIF Editor, 97, 225
Planisoft, 96, 213
Ports Icon, 158
Powerpoint, 211
Presentation graphics, 211
Print Manager, 147
Print Screen, 163
Printer installation, 27
Printer problems, 128
Printers
    activating, 156
    adding, 152
    changing, 152
    paper size, 154
    removing, 152
    Timeouts, 154
Printers Icon, 152
Printing
    cancelling, 150
    changing order, 150
    changing speed, 150
    interrupting, 150
    resuming, 150
    stopping, 150
Printing from Windows, 36
Program Manager, 32, 41, 73, 142
    File, Delete, 144, 145
    File, Exit Windows, 38
    File, Move, 146
    File, New, 143, 144, 171
    File, Properties, 143, 170
    File, Run, 230
    Window, 52, 55, 73
    Window, Arrange Icons, 146
Project, 213
Project management, 213

Q

Quitting Windows, 37

R

Radio buttons, 81
README.TXT, 80
Real mode, 34, 229
Real mode, forcing, 35
Recorder, 97, 110
    File, Open, 118
    File, Save, 113
    Macro, Record, 110
Renaming groups, 143
Restore button
    See Maximise button
Restoring a window, 50
Restoring from an icon, 51
Reversi, 52
Right clicking, 46
Root directory, 79

S

Screen capture, 163
Scroll arrows, 82
Scroll bars, 43, 78, 82
Scroll boxes, 82
SDK, 214
Selecting files, 138
Setup program, 20
Sizing a window, 67
SMARTDRV.SYS, 33
Solitaire, 40, 52
Sound Icon, 161
Spreadsheets, 204
SQL, 209, 219
SQL Connect, 219
Standard mode, 34
Starting Windows, 32
Sub-directories, 78
Superbase, 40, 64, 96, 123, 170,
    205, 206, 210, 214, 219
Supercalc, 204
Swapfiles, 229
System menu, 37, 43
SYSTEM.INI, 134, 228

Index

T

Task List, 60
Temporary files, 34
Terminal, 96, 226
Text
  entering, 83
  inserting, 84
  moving within, keyboard, 84
  moving within, mouse, 83
  overtyping, 84
  selecting, 84, 85
  working with, 83
Text boxes, 76
Tiling, 64
Tiling horizontally, 65
Time management, 213
Timeouts setting, 29
Title bar, 43
Toggles, 75
Toolbook, 214
Type Manager, 217

U

UNIX, 11, 12, 218
Utilities, 220

V

Ventura, 7, 64, 98, 202
Virtual memory, 229

W

Wallpaper, 160
WIMP, 12
WIN.INI, 97, 228
Window, components of, 42
Windows 2, 11
Windows 286, 11
Windows 3, launch, 13
Windows 386, 11
Windows Applications group, 42, 55, 95
Windows CAD, 211
Windows Express, 220
Windows Setup, 165
  Options, 165
Wingz, 96, 204
Word for Windows, 7, 64, 95, 199, 201, 210
Word processors, 197
WordPerfect, 11
WordPerfect for Windows, 199
Workspace, 43
Write, 95, 114, 188, 199
  Character, 191
  Character, Bold, 116
  Character, Fonts, 116, 128
  Document Footer, 192
  Document Header, 192
  Document, Page Layout, 191
  Document, Ruler On, 189
  Document, Tabs, 192
  Edit, Move Picture, 126
  Edit, Paste, 120, 121, 123, 124,
  Edit, Size Picture, 127
  Edit, Undo (Formatting), 191
  File, Open, 119, 188
  File, Print, 127, 193
  File, Repaginate, 192
  File, Save, 117, 127
  Paragraph, 189
  Paragraph, Centered, 116, 189
  Paragraph, Normal, 189
  Paragraphs, Indents, 190
  Search, 192
  Search, Go To, 192
WYSIWYG, 216

X

Xenix, 218